Colonial Williamsburg

A POCKET GUIDE

Essential Information
for Touring the Historic Area

The Colonial Williamsburg Foundation
Williamsburg, Virginia

© 2011 by The Colonial Williamsburg Foundation
All rights reserved. Published 2011

20 19 18 17 16 15 14 13 12 11   1 2 3 4 5 6 7 8 9

Printed in China

Library of Congress Cataloging-in-Publication Data

Colonial Williamsburg : a pocket guide.
    p. cm.
  Includes index.
  ISBN 978-0-87935-248-6 (pbk. : alk. paper) 1. Colonial
Williamsburg (Williamsburg, Va.)--Guidebooks. 2. Williamsburg
(Va.)--Guidebooks. 3. Historic sites--Interpretive programs--
Virginia--Williamsburg. I. Colonial Williamsburg Foundation. II. Title.

  F234.W7C65 2010
  975.5'4252--dc22

                                    2010031358

Designed by Helen M. Olds

Colonial Williamsburg®, Revolutionary City®, Colonial Williamsburg
Historic Trades®, WILLIAMSBURG At Home®, WILLIAMSBURG
Booksellers®, WILLIAMSBURG Celebrations™, WILLIAMSBURG
Revolutions™, Christiana Campbell's Tavern®, Chowning's Tavern®,
King's Arms Tavern®, Shields Tavern®, and Williamsburg Inn® are
marks of The Colonial Williamsburg Foundation, a not-for-profit
educational institution.

The Colonial Williamsburg Foundation
PO Box 1776
Williamsburg, VA 23187-1776
www.history.org

CONTENTS

WELCOME

When you come to Williamsburg, you are entering not just another place but another time. You are surrounded by the sights and sounds of the eighteenth century.

Here you'll see the opulent Governor's Palace, the embodiment of British order in the colonies; the Capitol, which witnessed America's move to independence; homes of the

gentry, the "middling sort," and enslaved people; an eighteenth-century farm; eighteenth-century gardens, both decorative and functional; and historic trades shops such as the blacksmith's where you'll hear the clanging of hammers and smell the coal-burning forges.

You won't just walk the same streets as Thomas Jefferson, George Washington, and Patrick Henry—you will walk right alongside them. Costumed interpreters render in first person the people who built our nation—famous and not, men and women, free and enslaved, European and African and Native American. Colonial Williamsburg's Revolutionary City street theater

4

program brings alive the drama of the period, when subjects of a king became citizens of a free republic.

And more: see rare breeds of sheep, cattle, horses, and fowl that populate Williamsburg's pastures and backyards; learn an eighteenth-century dance step; take part in a witch trial; march with the Fifes and Drums.

Nor will you want to miss the distinctive collections of the DeWitt Wallace Decorative Arts Museum and the Abby Aldrich Rockefeller Folk Art Museum. Here you can linger over singular examples of American and British antiques from the seventeenth, eighteenth, and nineteenth centuries and discover bold and imaginative works of colonial and contemporary folk art.

Here, too, are taverns, still gathering places for good food, conversation, and entertainment; shops where you can

buy reproductions of the items sold in Williamsburg's colonial-era stores and some of the exquisite hand-crafted work created by Colonial Williamsburg's tradespeople today; a unique spa inspired by centuries of wellness practices; award-winning golf courses; and hotels offering deluxe accommodations and unsurpassed value.

OPERATING HOURS

Open 365 days a year. Historic Area sites are generally open 9 a.m. to 5 p.m. with special programming in the evening.

Pick up a current copy of "THIS WEEK" at the Visitor Center or other ticket office. This free weekly guide will provide you with a daily listing of schedules and programs in the Historic Area as well as a full map.

A Brief History

Williamsburg was the thriving capital of Virginia when the dream of American freedom and independence was taking shape and the colony was a rich and powerful land stretching west to the Mississippi River and north to the Great Lakes. From 1699 to 1780, Williamsburg was the political, cultural, and educational center of what was then the largest, most populous, and most influential of the North American mainland colonies. It was here that the fundamental concepts of our republic—responsible leadership, a sense of public service, self-government, and individual liberty—were nurtured under the leadership of patriots such as George Washington, Thomas Jefferson, George Mason, and Peyton Randolph.

Near the end of the Revolutionary War and through the influence of Thomas Jefferson, the seat of government of Virginia was moved up the peninsula to the safer and more centrally located city of Richmond. For nearly a century and a half afterward, Williamsburg was a quiet town, home of the College of William and Mary and a hospital for the mentally ill.

In 1926, the Reverend Dr. W.A.R. Goodwin, rector of Bruton Parish Church, shared his dream of preserving the city's historic buildings with philanthropist John D. Rockefeller Jr., and the restoration began.

Goodwin feared that scores of structures that had figured in the life of the colony and the founding of the nation would soon disappear forever. Rockefeller and Goodwin began a modest project to preserve a few of the more important buildings. Eventually, the work progressed and expanded to include a major portion of the colonial town, encompassing approximately 85 percent of the eighteenth-century capital's original area.

Rockefeller gave the project his personal leadership until his death in 1960. He funded the preservation of more than eighty of the original structures, the reconstruction of many buildings, and also the construction of extensive facilities to accommodate the visiting public.

GETTING HERE

For someone living near Charlottesville, as Thomas Jefferson did, Williamsburg was four days away. By horse, that is. It's far more likely you'll be arriving by car.

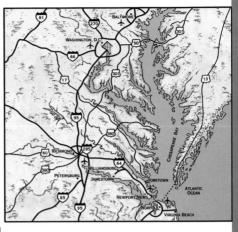

Williamsburg is midway between Richmond and Norfolk on Interstate 64. Take exit 238 and then follow the signs to the Colonial Williamsburg Visitor Center. The Visitor Center is located on highway 132Y. The physical address is 101A Visitor Center Drive. Once you purchase your admission pass, you can either take the shuttle bus or walk to Colonial Williamsburg's Historic Area. Cars are not permitted in the Historic Area.

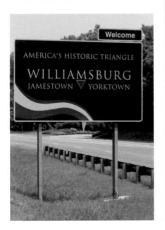

Convenient access via major airlines is just twenty-five to forty-five minutes away at Newport News-Williamsburg International Airport (PHF), Norfolk International Airport (ORF), and Richmond International Airport (RIC). Each has rental car and limousine services.

Amtrak and Greyhound serve the Williamsburg Transportation Center. The center is just blocks from the Historic Area and provides car rentals and a cab stand.

The twenty-three-mile Colonial Parkway connects Williamsburg to Jamestown and Yorktown, the other points of America's Historic Triangle.

VISITOR CENTER

Begin your visit at the Visitor Center, where you'll find ample free parking, restrooms, and information and reservation services. Purchase your tickets and get a current copy of "This Week," a free weekly guide to schedules and programs and map of the Historic Area. From here, it's a short bus ride to the Historic Area or walk a quarter mile across the pedestrian bridge, through Great Hopes Plantation, and into the Historic Area. Along the bridge are plaques marking your trip back in time. Before setting out, you might want to view the seven-minute orientation program *Where Do We Begin?* which is shown continuously.

If you're in a hurry to get started, by all means head off to the Historic Area. But, if you don't see it before you leave the Visitor Center, make sure to come back for *Williamsburg—The Story of a Patriot.* This is not your typical orientation film. Its director, writer, cast, and crew were all Academy Award winners. The movie stars a young Jack Lord as a fictional planter through whose eyes you see unfolding the tensions leading up to the American Revolution. The thirty-six-minute movie opened in 1957 and has been shown daily since, the longest run in motion picture history. The digitally restored version premiered in 2004. *Patriot* was shot in VistaVision, the first ultra-wide-screen film format. The theaters at the Visitor Center were created to further maximize the visual impact.

To view the film in a language other than English, please call ahead or give the Visitor Center staff one hour's notice of your language preference. You can choose from Spanish, French, German, Italian, Japanese, Portuguese, and Russian. Accommodations can also be made for guests with hearing impairments. Please ask the usher for assistance.

TOURING THE HISTORIC AREA

The Historic Area of Colonial Williamsburg stretches over 301 acres and includes eighty-eight original eighteenth-century structures. Hundreds of other houses, shops, public buildings, and outbuildings are reconstructed on their original foundations. Some buildings are open to the public while others are private residences and administrative offices. Some sites you tour in a small group led by an interpreter; some you tour on your own, but interpreters will be available to answer questions.

Not all sites are open every day, and not all sites are open all day. You can find the schedule on the map in "This Week." A British flag near a building's entrance also indicates that the site, store, or tavern is open.

Sites that require tickets are shown on the map in red and usually staffed at the entrance by a costumed interpreter, but, if a flag is present, ticketed guests should feel free to enter.

Although the streets and most gardens of the Historic Area are open to the general public, except during special programming, an admission ticket is required for access to Colonial Williamsburg exhibition sites, art museums, and daytime programs. Various options are available, including single-day, multiple-day, and year-round passes. An admission ticket includes access to *Williamsburg—The Story of a Patriot* and use of the Colonial Williamsburg shuttle buses, which circle the Historic Area. Evening programs and some other events require a separate ticket.

Duke of Gloucester Street is the main street in the Historic Area. It runs nearly a mile from the Wren Building at the

9

College of William and Mary at one end to the Capitol at the other end. Francis Street runs parallel to Duke of Gloucester Street on one side, and Nicolson Street runs parallel on the other side. The greatest number of exhibition sites is on Duke of Gloucester Street with some sites on Francis, Nicholson, and the intersecting streets.

An Orientation Walking Tour is also included in your admission ticket. Tours are conducted daily from 9 a.m. to 1 p.m. and leave about every fifteen minutes. They start at the Gateway Building and last about thirty minutes. These walks are designed to give you a general history of eighteenth-century Williamsburg and a basic overview of the Historic Area. Other walking tours are also available; check for tours at any ticket sales location.

To purchase tickets or for more information, go to the Visitor Center, the Lumber House Ticket Office, or the Merchants Square Ticket Office; visit the Colonial Williamsburg Web site at www .history.org/admission; or call 1-800-HISTORY (447-8679). You can also make lodging and dining reservations and purchase evening program tickets at the ticket offices or by calling 1-800-HISTORY. Audio tours are also available.

Cameras and recording equipment are permitted for personal use unless they interfere with interpretations and programs. In such cases, guests will be asked not to use them.

TICKET SALES LOCATIONS
• Visitor Center
• Lumber House Ticket Office
• Merchants Square Ticket Office
• Art Museums of Colonial Williamsburg Gift Shop
• Colonial Williamsburg Inn and Lodge (for hotel guests)

INCLUDED IN YOUR ADMISSION TICKET
• exhibition buildings
• regular daytime programming
• *Williamsburg—The Story of a Patriot*
• shuttle buses
• orientation tour

REVOLUTIONARY CITY
TICKET REQUIRED

Outdoor drama that brings alive the events of the American Revolution in Williamsburg.

Revolutionary City takes place at the eastern end of the Historic Area, near the Capitol, from mid-March until Thanksgiving, weather permitting, in the morning in the summer and in the afternoon in the spring and fall. The entire program runs for approximately ninety minutes daily. (See "This Week" for specific times.) Each of three days presents a different program. While each day's program tells a full story of a particular period of time, each scene stands alone so you need not see them in order or even see every one. The scenes run between ten and twenty minutes each.

WHAT HAPPENS HERE

Momentous events occurred in Williamsburg during the Revolutionary period, and Colonial Williamsburg's Revolutionary City brings them alive again on the streets where they actually took place. Guests participate with "colonial" townspeople in the events that led to independence and to the creation of a new kind of society, one in which subjects of a monarch became citizens of an independent republic. The program features both large-scale street theater events and multiple simultaneous vignettes, casting you in the midst of the American Revolution.

You may run into Virginia's historical giants such as Thomas Jefferson, George Washington, or Patrick Henry. You may also run into lesser-known figures, such as Barbry Hoy, wife of a soldier who was captured during the siege at Charleston; or Eve, an enslaved woman who debates with other African Americans about whether freedom can best be found by escaping behind British lines; or Gowan Pamphlet, a black Baptist preacher who expresses his hopes for a future when there is no state religion and when all people are considered citizens and treated equally.

Collapse of the Royal Government—1765–1776, which runs Tuesdays, Thursdays, and Saturdays, focuses on the prewar years when British policy, especially related to taxation, drastically alters the relationship between Great Britain and her North American colonies. Policies constructed by Parliament and supported by King George III drive the colonies toward declaring independence. During the Stamp Act riot of October 1765, gentlemen and merchants take to the streets to protest the tax imposed by Parliament. The story then advances to the time following the Boston Tea Party when colonists find themselves confronting not just wrongful taxation but also the removal of basic civil liberties that they have always held as British subjects. Guests experience the turmoil of arming and preparing for war, the anxieties suffered by the enslaved as they debate whether to leave their homes and families and accept a British offer of freedom in exchange for taking up arms against their masters, and the human dramas of families torn apart by divided loyalties. The day concludes with Virginia's leaders announcing their resolution for independence, which motivates the Continental Congress to break all ties with Great Britain.

Citizens at War—1776–1781 plays Wednesdays, Fridays, and Sundays and shows the sacrifices and challenges citizens endure as the war for independence changes their lives and world forever. The day begins

with the arrival and celebration of the Declaration of Independence in Williamsburg, just a few weeks after Virginia's representatives adopted their own declaration of rights and constitution. The celebrations don't last long, however, as the city suffers through economic hardship and British occupation. Ultimately, Washington and his troops, along with their French allies, arrive in Williams-burg and prepare to march to Yorktown, the site of the Revolution's last major battle.

During the *Building a Nation* program on Mondays, guests can meet the men and women who built a nation. These include preachers, house servants, farmers, actors, and artisans, free and enslaved, as well as the likes of Washington and Jefferson and Henry.

PUBLIC BUILDINGS

Mere brick and mortar, and yet within them evolved the ideas that were catalysts to the American Revolution. The opulent Governor's Palace was the embodiment of British order in the colonies. The Capitol was witness to the vote for America's move to independence. The Magazine held the colony's guns and ammunition, making it more than just a symbol of self-reliance.

BRUTON PARISH EPISCOPAL CHURCH
ORIGINAL BUILDING

The church where the founding fathers worshipped.

TOURING THE SITE

The church continues to serve a congregation of almost two thousand members, but guests are invited to visit, docents answer questions, and services and concerts are open to the public. Open for touring all day Monday–Saturday (except for Wednesday 11 a.m. service and daily noonday prayer) and Sunday afternoon. Closed for touring during services and special church functions. No ticket is required but the church does request donations.

THE BUILDING

Bruton Parish Church was the first important public building in Williamsburg, as indicated by its location near the center of Williamsburg's original survey map of 1699. The first brick church was built in 1683. The present structure

was completed in 1715. Its cruciform shape arose less from religious symbolism than a desire to accommodate college and government personnel. The Reverend Dr. W. A. R. Goodwin spearheaded the church's restoration early in the twentieth century. Later, Goodwin played a key role in persuading John D. Rockefeller Jr. to fund the restoration of the rest of Williamsburg.

WHAT HAPPENED HERE

In colonial Virginia, there was no separation of church and state. The Church of England, which in America later became Episcopal, was the official church. Free Virginians were required by law to attend services at least once a month. Yet some Virginia Anglicans led the movement to disestablish the church.

Blacks also worshipped at Bruton Parish, though during the Revolution many formed a church of their own. A plaque on Nassau Street marks the site of what was known as the "African Church." Opposite that site is the Taliaferro-Cole Stable, which houses an exhibit on African-American religion.

THE PEOPLE
Thomas Jefferson, George Washington, Richard Henry Lee, George Wythe, Patrick Henry, George Mason, and other founding fathers worshipped here. Buried in the churchyard are first rector Rowland Jones and two infant children of Martha Custis Washington and her first husband. (In the eighteenth century, it was more typical to be buried at home in a private cemetery.) Jailer Peter Pelham was organist from 1768 until 1802.

CAPITOL
RECONSTRUCTED BUILDING
TICKET REQUIRED

Where elected leaders debated and ultimately declared independence, making Virginia the first colony to do so.

TOURING THE SITE
Interpreter-led tours run regularly and last about thirty minutes.

THE BUILDING
The original Capitol was completed in 1705. That building burned down in 1747. The second Capitol was completed in 1753. In 1832, it too was destroyed by fire. The current Capitol, reconstructed in 1934, was built on the foundations of the original building and based on a contemporary engraving of the 1705 building discovered in the 1920s.

The building is shaped like an H. The first floor was split between the House of Burgesses, which was the lower house of the legislature who were elected by Virginia's landowners, and the General Courtroom. The second floor was split between the burgesses' committee rooms and the Governor's Council chamber. The twelve Council members were appointed for life by the king. If the House and the Council deadlocked, representatives from each met in the second-floor conference room that was a literal bridge between the two wings.

WHAT HAPPENED HERE
The first elected assembly in British North America first met in Jamestown and then moved to Williamsburg. In May 1765, Patrick Henry protested the Stamp Act: "If this be treason, make the most of it!" In May 1774, the burgesses expressed their solidarity with the people of Boston after the Boston Tea Party by resolving to hold a day of fasting, humiliation, and prayer. Virginia's royal governor, Lord Dunmore, responded by disbanding the House. In May 1776, the burgesses instructed their delegates to the Continental Congress to propose independence. Virginia was the first colony to speak for independence. The next month, the burgesses adopted George Mason's Declaration of Rights.

The General Court also met here. It was the high court for the colony. In June and December, it heard criminal cases. In April and October, it heard both civil and criminal cases.

On December 24, 1779, the General Assembly met here for the last time; the capital moved to Richmond. But every other year since 1934, Virginia legislators reassemble for a day in the Capitol.

THE PEOPLE
At this site, Patrick Henry, Thomas Jefferson, George Washington, George Mason, and George Wythe, among others, debated the issues that ultimately led to American independence, to Mason's Declaration of Rights, and to Jefferson's bill for religious freedom. Of the first five presidents of the United States, four began their government careers here.

COURTHOUSE
ORIGINAL BUILDING
TICKET REQUIRED

At the very center of the city, the Courthouse was also central to the systems of local government and justice.

TOURING THE SITE
Interpreters introduce you to

the site and answer questions. During reenactments of actual eighteenth-century trials, you can become a defendant, witness, or justice.

THE BUILDING
Standing near the center of the city on Market Square, the Courthouse was built in 1770–1771. The building's formal design elements—round-headed windows, a cantilevered pediment, and an octagonal cupola—reinforce the building's official appearance. The double doors open directly into the courtroom. Columns were added early in the twentieth century but later removed to restore the building to its eighteenth-century appearance.

WHAT HAPPENED HERE
Colonial Virginia's courts acted as the principal agents of local government. They handled petty crimes and civil cases as well as any crimes committed by enslaved persons. Here were heard the debtor's dispute with his creditor, the accusations against the pig stealer, the apprentice's pleas for protection from an abusive master, and the white man's complaint of a slave's thievery. Punishment was quick; the whipping post and the public stocks stand just outside. (You can try them out yourself.) Serious cases involving free subjects were the province of the General Court, which met each April and October in the Capitol. This courthouse served both James City County and the city of Williamsburg.

GOVERNOR'S PALACE
RECONSTRUCTED BUILDING
TICKET REQUIRED

Home to seven royal governors and the first two governors of the independent Commonwealth of Virginia, Patrick Henry and Thomas Jefferson.

TOURING THE SITE
Interpreter-led tours of the building start regularly and run about thirty minutes. Tour gardens and grounds on your own.

THE BUILDING AND GROUNDS
Construction began in 1705

and proceeded fitfully (and expensively, to the increasing exasperation of the House of Burgesses) for almost twenty years. Even after that, alterations continued to be made. Ultimately, the building measured up to the name of "Palace," certainly compared to other colonial structures. The five-bay Georgian home stands inside gates—guarded by a stone unicorn on one side and a stone lion on the other—along with two brick advance buildings. Visitors who called on the king's representative in Virginia passed through the gates and forecourt, up the stone steps, and into a hall where an imposing display of muskets, swords, and pistols signaled they had arrived at the seat of power.

Beyond the house are formal gardens. A mound of earth covering the eighteenth-century icehouse remains today, and guests can stand on it to look

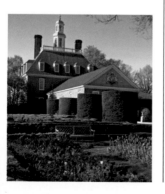

out on grounds that stretch to the north. The stable, carriage house, kitchen, scullery, laundry, and octagonal bathhouse are arranged in service yards beside the advance buildings. At the kitchen today, Historic Foodways staff demonstrate the eighteenth-century high style of cooking.

The Palace was destroyed by fire in 1781. It was meticulously reconstructed based on archaeological investigations, drawings by Thomas Jefferson, General Assembly records, and a copperplate engraving discovered in England's Bodleian Library in 1929.

WHAT HAPPENED HERE

The Palace hosted numerous festive balls celebrating events ranging from the king's birthday to the arrival of a Cherokee chief to sign a treaty. Instructed to win over rebellious Virginia planters, Governor Norborne Berkeley, Baron de Botetourt, received fifty-two dinner guests one day and expected as many more the next.

The last royal governor of Virginia, Lord Dunmore, turned the Palace into a garrison to protect himself from townspeople infuriated by his removal of the gunpowder from the magazine. On June 8, 1775, he fled under cover of darkness, never to return. The

Palace muskets and swords were pulled down by local men and carried to the magazine.

General Charles Lee of the Continental army made the Palace his headquarters. Then Virginia's government ordered the building renovated for the commonwealth's governors. The Palace served as a hospital in the fall of 1781 for American soldiers wounded in the Battle of Yorktown. Some 156 of them are buried in the garden along with two women who were probably nurses.

THE PEOPLE

Seven royal governors—Alexander Spotswood; Hugh Drysdale; William Gooch; Robert Dinwiddie; Francis Fauquier; Norborne Berkeley, Baron de Botetourt; and John Murray, Earl of Dunmore—and the commonwealth's first two governors—Patrick Henry and Thomas Jefferson—lived here. The Palace is furnished as it was when Dunmore and his wife and six of their seven children occupied it. Inventories of personal property attest to the elaborate furnishings of a household that required approximately twenty-five servants and slaves, including stewards, personal servants, butlers, footmen, cooks, laundresses, gardeners, maids, grooms, and laborers.

MAGAZINE AND GUARDHOUSE
ORIGINAL AND RECONSTRUCTED BUILDINGS
TICKET REQUIRED

The spark that ignited the Revolution in Virginia was struck here.

TOURING THE SITE

Tour on your own, though interpreters are available to answer questions. Besides viewing original and reproduction arms and other military equipment, you sometimes can watch firing demonstrations or even join in a drill conducted by a militia sergeant.

THE BUILDINGS

The Magazine was erected in 1715 after Governor Alexander Spotswood requested a building to store the colony's arms and ammunitions. Spotswood himself is usually credited with the Magazine's unusual octagonal design.

Because so much gunpowder was stored here, the residents of Williamsburg later constructed a high wall around the building and a guardhouse nearby. After the government moved to Richmond, the Magazine became, successively, a market, a Baptist meetinghouse, a Confederate arsenal, a dancing school, and a livery stable.

WHAT HAPPENED HERE

On the night of April 20, 1775, royal seamen stole toward the capital. Their orders, straight from Lord Dunmore, the royal governor, were to empty the arsenal and disable the muskets stored there. Spotted by some local residents, the seamen fled in the dark with fifteen half barrels of powder. Most of Williamsburg's population gathered on Market Square, and some talked of doing Dunmore harm. Peyton Randolph, Robert Carter Nicholas, and Mayor John Dixon calmed the crowd. Less than a week after the raid

on the Magazine, word reached Williamsburg of a remarkably similar attempt to seize arms and ammunition in Massachusetts, which led to fighting at Lexington and Concord. In early June, rumors that royal forces were returning brought out the militia. On June 8, Dunmore fled to a British ship, ending British rule in Virginia.

PUBLIC GAOL
ORIGINAL BUILDING
TICKET REQUIRED

Prison conditions were harsh. Note, for example, the shackles in the cells and the steps up to the hole that served as a toilet.

TOURING THE SITE

Enter through the jail keeper's parlor for a brief introduction, and then tour the yard and cells on your own.

THE BUILDING

Legislation passed in 1701 called for the construction of

a "substantiall Brick Prison." The act also called for a walled exercise yard. Two cells were opened in 1704, and debtors' cells were added in 1711. The Gaol has been restored to the way it looked in 1722 and includes quarters for the jailer and his family.

WHAT HAPPENED HERE
Few prisoners were held here for long. Most waited for a quarterly session of the General Court or the Court of Oyer and Terminer, after which those found guilty were generally branded, whipped, or hanged. Though sentences were harsh by modern standards, first offenders might expect mercy, and some miscreants were merely fined.

THE PEOPLE
The Public Gaol confined criminals, debtors, runaway slaves, and occasionally the mentally ill. During the Revolution, Tories, spies, military prisoners, deserters, and traitors were among the prisoners. The Gaol's most celebrated occupants were fifteen henchmen of the pirate Blackbeard, caught in 1718. Thirteen were hanged, one was acquitted, and one, Israel Hands, was pardoned after testifying against the rest. Hands's stories about Blackbeard may have inspired Robert Louis Stevenson's *Treasure Island*. Henry "Hair Buyer" Hamilton, the royal governor of British Detroit, was held here after he was captured in 1779. Hamilton was accused of buying pioneers' scalps from Indians. The best-known jail keeper was Peter Pelham, who was also organist at Bruton Parish Church, clerk of the Governor's Council, and a local theater producer.

PUBLIC HOSPITAL
RECONSTRUCTED BUILDING
TICKET REQUIRED

The first building in America devoted solely to the treatment of individuals with mental disorders.

TOURING THE SITE
Tour on your own. Some aspects of this exhibit may be disturbing to children. The entrance to the Public Hospital also serves as entrance to the DeWitt Wallace Decorative Arts Museum and the Abby Aldrich Rockefeller Folk Art Museum.

THE BUILDING

The building, which opened in 1773, originally housed twenty-four cells for patients. Each cell had a mattress, a chamber pot, an iron ring in the wall to which the patient's wrist or leg fetters were attached, and a stout door with a barred window that looked out onto a dim central passage. A fire completely destroyed the original building on June 7, 1885. It was reconstructed in 1985.

WHAT HAPPENED HERE

The first "persons of insane and disordered minds" were admitted in 1773. Only those considered dangerous or curable were admitted. Treatment originally consisted of restraint, strong drugs, plunge baths, bleeding, and blistering salves. Given the treatments administered, the hospital had a surprising success rate: of the forty-two patients admitted between 1773 and 1779, ten were discharged as "restored." Treatments changed over the years, becoming more kindly, in accordance with current best practice.

Today you can view cells that trace the evolution of treatment of mental illness. A 1773 cell is prisonlike; an 1845 apartment more comfortable and domestic. An accompanying exhibit provides additional perspective on the history of the institution and the methods of treating mental illness. Eighteenth- and nineteenth-century artifacts include lancets for bloodletting, syringes for purging the body of supposedly harmful fluids, and an electrostatic generator used to shock patients. Many of the artifacts were recovered at the site by archaeologists.

THE PEOPLE

In 1766, Royal Governor Francis Fauquier first proposed the hospital saying, "Every civilized Country has an Hospital for these People, where they are confined, maintained and attended by able Physicians, to endeavour to restore to them their lost Reason." The original staff consisted of Dr. John de Sequeyra, a physician educated in Holland; James Galt, former jail keeper; and John's wife, Mary Galt.

WREN BUILDING
ORIGINAL BUILDING

The oldest academic structure in America and still used for classes and faculty offices at the College of William and Mary.

Touring the Site
Tour on your own.

The Building

Construction began in 1695, two years after King William III and Queen Mary II granted a royal charter for a college in the colony of Virginia. The Reverend Hugh Jones, a William and Mary professor, wrote in 1724 that the building was "modelled by Sir Christopher Wren," and scholars continue to debate what role the famed British architect played in designing it. Three times damaged by fire, the building has often changed in appearance but today looks much as it did in 1732.

WHAT HAPPENED HERE

In its early years, the building housed students and contained classrooms, a refectory or dining hall, a library, a faculty room, and living quarters for the president and masters. A kitchen and servants' rooms were located in the basement. Students who enrolled in the college received a classical education. From the east entrance to the Wren Building, you can see the other buildings of the colonial campus, including the Brafferton, which was constructed in 1723 to house the College's school for Indian boys, and the President's House, which was erected in 1732–1733 and has been used by every president of William and Mary since then. The Brafferton and the President's House are not open to the public.

THE PEOPLE

Thomas Jefferson, James Monroe, John Tyler, and John Marshall studied in the rooms of this building. Jefferson began his studies here in 1760 at the age of sixteen and remained just over two years. He didn't receive a degree, which at the time was considered unnecessary. George Washington was once chancellor of the college. Most of the William and Mary students left the college when the Revolution began. During the Battle of Yorktown, the building served as a hospital.

TAVERNS AND COFFEEHOUSE

Taverns and coffeehouses were places to eat (and, in the case of taverns, sleep), discuss business, hear the latest news and gossip, debate, and sometimes determine the political future of America. The three sites below are exhibition sites, but Colonial Williamsburg does offer historic lodging and dining options in restored taverns (see pages 78–79 and 82).

CHARLTON'S COFFEEHOUSE
RECONSTRUCTED BUILDING
TICKET REQUIRED

Opened in 2009, this reconstructed site is the Historic Area's only coffeehouse. This is an exhibition site, not a working coffeehouse, though tours do include samples of coffee, tea, or "chocolate" (a hot drink) made in the style of the times.

TOURING THE SITE
Interpreter-led tours run regularly and last about twenty minutes.

THE BUILDING
Based on extensive archaeological research and rebuilt with eighteenth-century building materials and methods, Richard Charlton's Coffeehouse is the only eighteenth-century coffeehouse in the nation. Archaeological research not only indicated what the building looked like but how it was used. A layer of more than ten thousand artifacts found near the porch was made up primarily of fragments of wine bottles and tobacco pipe stems, and bones found nearby indicated that the coffeehouse served veal, mutton, opossum, and even peacocks.

WHAT HAPPENED HERE
Like the historic taverns in the Historic Area, a coffeehouse was a place to gather and hear the latest news—all the more so because of its location next to the Capitol. Unlike taverns, coffeehouses didn't offer lodging, so they had a reputation as more genteel establishments.

In the fall of 1765, a crowd protesting the Stamp Act cornered George Mercer, the chief distributor of stamps in Virginia and essentially the collector of a hated tax. Governor Francis Fauquier witnessed the riot from the porch of Charlton's Coffeehouse and escorted

Mercer to safety. Mercer ended up resigning his position, and Parliament repealed the Stamp Act the next year, but the incident provided a taste of the Revolution to come.

THE PEOPLE

Richard Charlton, a wigmaker, opened the coffeehouse in the early 1760s. The coffeehouse was frequented by merchants and gentry like George Washington and Thomas Jefferson as well as Governor Fauquier. Still, the coffeehouse was not a financial success, partly because of the economic downturn that followed the French and Indian War and maybe also because people tended to sit a long time without buying much. Charlton converted the coffeehouse to a tavern in 1767.

RALEIGH TAVERN
RECONSTRUCTED BUILDING
TICKET REQUIRED

The place to meet—whether for social, commercial, or political gatherings.

TOURING THE SITE

Open for scheduled programs only. See "This Week" for programs. The Raleigh Tavern Bakery, just behind the tavern, is a convenient stop for a snack. (No ticket required for the bakery.)

THE BUILDING

Established in 1717, the tavern grew in size and reputation through the years. It was named after Sir Walter Raleigh, who attempted the first colonization of Virginia. The Raleigh offered food, drink, and lodging. The tavern burned down in 1859 and was rebuilt between 1928 and 1932.

WHAT HAPPENED HERE

Painted in gilt above the mantel of the tavern's Apollo Room are Latin words that translate to "Jollity, the offspring of wisdom and good living." There were often balls and dancing at the Raleigh, and planters and merchants often gathered at its bar (which is literally behind bars). There were more serious gatherings here as well. In 1774, for example, after royal governor Lord Dunmore dissolved the House of Burgesses for objecting to the closing of Boston's port after its Tea Party, eighty-nine burgesses reassembled at the Raleigh.

THE PEOPLE

The tavern's central location made it a center of political activity, but (one suspects) so did the sympathies of its proprietor, James Southall. Eighteen slaves helped run the busy tavern.

WETHERBURN'S TAVERN

ORIGINAL BUILDING
TICKET REQUIRED

One of Williamsburg's most thoroughly restored sites.

TOURING THE SITE

Interpreter-led tours run regularly and last about twenty-five minutes. Please note that the interpreters at this site are not in colonial dress.

THE BUILDING

A detailed inventory of Henry Wetherburn's personal property, dated just a month after his death in 1760, was used to refurnish his tavern, an original building. The inventory also provided valuable information about the type of services he offered his customers and the use of each room. Various outbuildings and a garden complete the property.

WHAT HAPPENED HERE

Merriment and conviviality were the specialties of the house. So popular was the tavern that around 1750 Wetherburn added the "great room" with additional space for entertaining his guests. Though the sleeping quarters were comfortable by eighteenth-century standards, Wetherburn's guests—like those at other taverns in town—had to share beds and some slept on the floor.

THE PEOPLE

Wetherburn's interest in taverns and women were closely intertwined. His first wife, Mary Bowcock, was widow of the keeper of the Raleigh Tavern, and Wetherburn first worked as keeper there. Ten days after Mary died, Henry married Anne Marot Ingles Shields, widow of tavern keeper James Shields and daughter of tavern keeper John Marot. Wetherburn owned twelve to fourteen enslaved persons who provided the labor to run the tavern.

HOUSES

Wander through the homes of the gentry and the middling sort, filled with period furnishings and costumed interpreters, and witness the worlds of both free and enslaved people.

THOMAS EVERARD HOUSE
ORIGINAL BUILDING
TICKET REQUIRED

A fashionable home for a fashionable location on Palace Green.

TOURING THE SITE
Interpreter-led tours run regularly and last about forty-five minutes. Please note that the interpreters at this site are not in colonial dress.

THE BUILDING
The house is noted for its fine staircase with its elaborately turned balusters, sweeping handrails, and richly ornamented carvings. It was originally built in 1718 by John Brush as a typical timber-framed one-and-one-half-story building. A section of the original roofing is still in place. It was later enlarged and embellished to reflect the affluence of its 1755 owner, Thomas Everard. Two wings were added to the back, resulting in the U-shaped design. Fragments of original wallpaper and paint provided information about the house's eighteenth-century appearance. The smokehouse and the

kitchen on the property are also original buildings.

THE PEOPLE
Brush was a gunsmith and armorer. Everard arrived in Virginia as an orphan apprentice in the 1730s and became a wealthy and respected local leader, twice serving as mayor of Williamsburg. Everard's nineteen slaves lived behind the house above the kitchen, laundry, and stable.

JAMES GEDDY HOUSE
ORIGINAL BUILDING
TICKET REQUIRED

Home of a prominent silversmith and his family. A favorite site for families since children can see how the children lived and play with toys like hoops and ninepins.

TOURING THE SITE
Interpreter-led tours run

regularly and last about fifteen minutes. You can then visit the family businesses behind the house, the foundry and the gunsmith, or you can see them separately.

THE BUILDING

James Geddy Jr. built the two-story house shortly after 1762. The L-shape was uncommon in Williamsburg and may have been adapted to fit the corner lot. The low-pitched roof, lack of dormers, and balcony are also unusual features. The reconstructed porch shows the tendency of colonial builders to mix different architectural styles.

WHAT HAPPENED HERE

James Geddy Jr. tore down his family's home on this site and built the current house, which provided a more stately and dignified image for the public figure he wished to be. Geddy's customers were gentry, and he himself acquired some wealth and influence. In addition to being a residence, the property also housed Geddy's retail and other family businesses, including a foundry and gunsmith.

THE PEOPLE

Geddy and his wife, Elizabeth, had five children: Mary, Anne, William, James, and Elizabeth. The children lived upstairs, as did a master silversmith named Galt. Anne Geddy's admirers included an anonymous poet whose work, published in the *Virginia Gazette* of December 22, 1768, was titled "*On Miss ANNE GEDDY singing, and playing on the* Spinet."

GREAT HOPES PLANTATION
RECONSTRUCTED BUILDINGS
TICKET REQUIRED

Most colonial Virginians were neither wellborn nor the "lesser sort" but rather "middling," and most lived on small plantations like Great Hopes.

TOURING THE SITE

Interpreters introduce you to the site and answer questions.

THE BUILDINGS

Great Hopes Plantation represents the many middling plantations that existed around the capital. Carpenters constructed the buildings at

Great Hopes using eighteenth-century tools and techniques. Slave houses at Great Hopes are much rougher than house-servant quarters in town.

WHAT HAPPENED HERE
Middling farmers and slaves generally grew tobacco, corn, wheat, and some cotton. They also tended livestock, including cattle, pigs, sheep, goats, and a few oxen and horses. You may see historic farmers and interpreters working at some of these same chores today.

THE PEOPLE
Great Hopes presents the lives of the working farmers and enslaved people who made up the majority of Virginians during the colonial era.

PEYTON RANDOLPH HOUSE
ORIGINAL BUILDING
TICKET REQUIRED

Home of one of Virginia's most prominent families and of the many slaves who worked in and behind the house.

TOURING THE SITE
Interpreter-led tours run regularly and last about forty-five minutes.

THE BUILDING
The Peyton Randolph House is one of the most handsome homes in Williamsburg. What were once two houses were linked in the mid-eighteenth century by a two-story central section featuring a grand stairway and a monumental round-headed window. Original paneling exists in several rooms as well as a marble mantle in the dining room. A full complement of reconstructed outbuildings stand in back, including a kitchen, stable, coach house, and dairy.

WHAT HAPPENED HERE

The Randolph family was torn apart by the Revolution, with Peyton Randolph supporting the patriot cause and brother John siding with the Crown. Betty Randolph continued to live in the house after her husband's death in 1775. Her home was used as the headquarters of the comte de Rochambeau in 1781 before the siege of Yorktown. Interpretation at the site also focuses on the lives of the enslaved people who lived and worked here and the choices they faced during the Revolution. Some chose to run away to nearby British forces.

THE PEOPLE

Peyton Randolph presided over every important Virginia Assembly in the years leading up to the Revolution. In Philadelphia, he was unanimously elected chairman of the Continental Congress—leading the British to place him on a list of those they proposed to hang. Before George Washington succeeded him as America's patriarch, Randolph was called the father of his country. He died in 1775.

Both Peyton and his brother John originally hoped for reconciliation with England. Once it was clear that reconciliation was unlikely, John sailed with his family back "home" to England in 1775. His son, Edmund, however, chose to remain in America as a patriot.

Among Peyton Randolph's twenty-seven slaves was Eve. Eve evidently responded to the British offer of freedom for slaves who deserted rebel masters since Randolph's probate inventory lists eight slaves from the estate as "gone to the enemy." Eve apparently was later forced to return, evidenced by a codicil to the will of Randolph's widow, Betty: "Eve's bad behaviour laid me under the necessity of selling her."

GEORGE WYTHE HOUSE
ORIGINAL BUILDING
TICKET REQUIRED

One of the grandest private homes in town, as befit one of the most influential Americans of his era.

TOURING THE SITE
Interpreters introduce you

to the site and answer questions. Then tour the home and grounds on your own. In the home you will see not only the living quarters of Mr. and Mrs. Wythe but also items that supported Mr. Wythe's various interests, especially law and science. You may meet the marquis de Lafayette or Patrick Henry or George Washington (who used the home as his headquarters prior to the siege of Yorktown).

THE BUILDING

Considered the finest private residence in eighteenth-century Williamsburg, the two-story brick residence is believed to have been designed in the mid-1750s by George Wythe's father-in-law Richard Taliaferro. Two great chimneys afford a fireplace in all eight rooms. A comprehensive study of wallpaper usage in colonial Virginia provided documentation for the striking patterns and colors used throughout. Behind the house are fine symmetrical gardens as well as reconstructed outbuildings, including a smokehouse, kitchen, laundry, poultry house, lumber house, well, dovecote, and stable.

WHAT HAPPENED HERE

Wythe moved into the house after he married Elizabeth Taliaferro around 1755. He lived here until 1791 when he moved to Richmond. (Elizabeth died in 1787.) Among those to whom George Wythe taught law in this house was Thomas Jefferson, who later referred to Wythe as "my faithful and beloved Mentor in youth, and my most affectionate friend through life." The house served as Washington's headquarters just before the siege of Yorktown.

THE PEOPLE

Though perhaps best known for teaching law to Jefferson and to future Supreme Court Chief Justice John Marshall, Wythe deserves to be known for his own achievements as a patriot leader. He was a member and then clerk of the House of Burgesses, one of Virginia's delegates to the Continental Congress, a signer of the Declaration of Independence, and a delegate to the Constitutional Convention. George Wythe opposed slavery in principle and freed some of his slaves during his lifetime.

HISTORIC TRADES

Working in period shops, using period techniques and tools to make re-creations of period products, Colonial Williamsburg's tradespeople not only present the lives of working men and women but also are among the best traditional artisans in the country.

VISITING THE TRADES SITES

Enter any open site and watch tradespeople create eighteenth-century items just as they did over two hundred years ago. Chat with the tradespeople at your leisure. They are fully versed in their disciplines both academically and practically, and, although they are dressed in colonial clothing and may use eighteenth-century terms, unlike some costumed interpreters in the Historic Area they do not portray eighteenth-century characters or speak in eighteenth-century dialects. True to eighteenth-century form, however, one master tradesperson oversees each trades shop. Under his or her direction, journeymen and women practice the trade and apprentices learn it. Come and go at the trades shops as you please.

APOTHECARY

(Pasteur & Galt Apothecary Shop)
RECONSTRUCTED BUILDING
TICKET REQUIRED

WHAT HAPPENS HERE

Unlike the eighteenth-century occupants of this shop, the interpreters at the Pasteur & Galt Apothecary Shop do not actually practice medicine. But they can tell you, sometimes in great detail, and often show you how it was practiced. The apothecary was also a druggist. British delft drug jars for storing medications line one wall, and antique implements for compounding and dispensing drugs are also displayed. Medication recipes in eighteenth-century pharmacy books show that some of the

ingredients that were used in colonial remedies are the basis for modern medications: chalk for heartburn, calamine for skin irritations, caffeine for headaches, and cinchona bark for fevers. The shop also features reproduction splints for broken bones, surgical tools, and dental tools. Some items

38

on display are original to the site. Williamsburg apothecaries also sold cooking spices, candles, salad oil, anchovies, toothbrushes, and tobacco, making them true precursors of today's drugstores.

THE PEOPLE

Two apothecary-surgeons, Dr. William Pasteur and Dr. John Galt, practiced at the Pasteur & Galt Apothecary Shop from 1775 to 1778. Both apprenticed in Williamsburg and then studied at Saint Thomas's Hospital in London. The shop features copies of Dr. Galt's certificates from Saint Thomas's Hospital for training completed in surgery. He also trained elsewhere in medical theory and midwifery.

BASKETMAKER
(on the George Wythe property)
TICKET REQUIRED

WHAT HAPPENS HERE

While basketmaking was an established trade in England during the eighteenth century, in Virginia it was a domestic activity practiced by the rural people who made up the bulk of the population. Boys and girls both learned to make baskets at an early age. Baskets are made from white oak trees that are about six to eight inches in diameter. Basketmakers start with a six-foot section of a green log and split it down its length a number of times. Then, using a knife, the basketmaker slices along the growth rings and peels away long, flexible "splits." The wooden splits are allowed to dry and are then woven into a variety of useful shapes and sizes. During the Revolution, American forces required vast numbers of standard-sized baskets. This demand led to the evolution of basketmaking into a skilled occupation.

BLACKSMITH
(James Anderson Blacksmith Shop and Public Armoury)
RECONSTRUCTED BUILDINGS
TICKET REQUIRED

THE BUILDINGS

Colonial Williamsburg is in the process of reconstructing this industrial site to reflect the complex that developed here in the late 1770s in support of the war effort—an armory,

a kitchen, a privy, two storage buildings, and a tinsmith's shop.

WHAT HAPPENS HERE

Though located in the heart of Williamsburg, Anderson's Blacksmith Shop and Public Armoury was an industrial site that reflected the complexity and urgency of mounting a war effort. Numerous trades worked together: blacksmiths forging and repairing weapons, tools, and hardware; gunsmiths repairing and rebuilding old guns; and tinsmiths fashioning all sorts of military accoutrements. The tinsmith's shop will be the only one of its kind in America to use eighteenth-century methods. During the archaeological and building phases, interpretation focuses on the research that goes into reconstructing a site and the construction of buildings as Colonial Williamsburg's archaeologists unearth the past and then tradespeople use eighteenth-century methods to prepare materials and hardware, lay foundations, and frame and finish the structures.

THE PEOPLE

James Anderson was appointed public armourer in 1776 by the General Assembly of the newly independent Virginia. Anderson immediately began to enlarge his small commercial blacksmithing operation into an extensive and diverse manufactury. At its peak, more than forty men worked here, including local smiths, French armorers, Scottish highlander prisoners of war, American soldiers, enslaved African Americans, and young men serving apprenticeships.

BRICKYARD
(open seasonally)
TICKET REQUIRED

Bricks were often made at or near building sites in the eighteenth century, but brickyards were also familiar to our colonial forebears. What you see today depends on what season you arrive. In the spring and summer, for example, brickmakers use their feet to mix clay and water and often invite guests to help. (Kids who like to get muddy love to get in the treading pit.) Then brickmakers mold the clay into bricks. In the fall, they stack about twenty thousand bricks to form a kiln and fire it up. Bricks made at the brickyard are used in building foundations, chimneys, walkways, and reconstructed buildings throughout the Historic Area.

CABINETMAKER
(Hay's Cabinetmaking Shop)
RECONSTRUCTED BUILDING
TICKET REQUIRED

WHAT HAPPENS HERE
Using traditional woods and designs, today's tradespeople produce furniture with colonial tools. They also practice the trade of harpsichord making, which was documented as one of the shop's offerings in 1767. In the eighteenth century, cabinetmakers produced fine furniture and musical instru-

ments that reflected Virginians' increasing wealth, though Virginians preferred "plain and neat" rather than the more decorative furniture popular in Philadelphia and Boston.

THE PEOPLE
One of the largest of the cabinetmaking shops in Williamsburg was Anthony Hay's, established by 1751 at this site. Among Hay's many employees were a Virginia-born apprentice, a London-trained journeyman cabinetmaker, a skilled slave cabinetmaker, and a master carver from London. The Hay shop produced a ceremonial chair for Virginia's governor and two more chairs for masters of Masonic lodges in Virginia. Hay gave up the business in 1766 to operate the Raleigh Tavern, after which he leased the building. Cabinetmakers Benjamin Bucktrout and Edmund Dickinson were two subsequent renters.

Historic Trades

CARPENTER AND JOINER
(Ayscough House)
RECONSTRUCTED BUILDING
TICKET REQUIRED

WHAT HAPPENS HERE
While often practiced by the same person, carpentry and joinery represent two different eighteenth-century trades. Carpenters work throughout the Historic Area and often prepare materials at Great Hopes Plantation. They reconstruct and repair buildings using eighteenth-century tools and techniques, building and raising frame buildings, nailing siding, and laying floors and shingles. At the Ayscough House, joiners, who might be called finish carpenters today, practice their trade, which involves constructing the

"joined" features of a building, such as doors, window sashes, mantels, and moldings. Joiners also build basic utilitarian pieces of furniture. Carpenters and joiners built the city in the eighteenth century, and they continue to do so today. The Public Armoury is the most recent major addition to the Historic Area raised by carpenters and joiners.

COOPER
(Ludwell-Paradise Stable)
RECONSTRUCTED BUILDING
TICKET REQUIRED

What Happens Here
Firkin, kilderkin, hogshead, butt, rundlet, tierce, puncheon, pipe, barrel: All these are names of casks of different sizes that were used to store and ship products ranging from gunpowder to tobacco, from butter to beer. Other "cooperage" that the cooper makes includes buckets, churns, and cups.

Coopers shape staves split from oak with axes, drawknives, and a cooper's jointer and then gather them into a circle secured by a metal ring. They heat the staves to make them pliant, bend them into shape, and hammer on the iron or wooden hoops. The trickiest step is cutting grooves inside the lips so the cask heads fit tightly. In an era before cardboard boxes or plastic buckets, casks were crucial. They were especially handy for shipping since they could be rolled. A fourteen-hundred-pound hogshead of tobacco, for example, was a common item shipped from Virginia to England with no modern machinery to move it.

FOODWAYS
(in the Governor's Palace kitchen and the Peyton Randolph House kitchen)
TICKET REQUIRED

WHAT HAPPENS HERE
From mince pies to syllabubs, members of Colonial Williamsburg's Foodways team re-create the dishes of the eighteenth century. Demonstrations based on eighteenth-century recipes and using eighteenth-century tools and methods occur at the Governor's Palace kitchen and the Peyton Randolph kitchen. Sometimes you can also see special programs on topics like brewing and chocolate making. Foods and preparation techniques varied, depending on the wealth and standing of the household. The Palace kitchen was run by European-trained chefs while gentry like the Randolphs depended on slaves who had little formal training but often were very skilled. Poor households often had just one pot, in which the woman of the house made soups and porridges. Guests are not allowed to sample the products at the Foodways demonstrations because of current health and safety regulations.

GARDENER
(Colonial Garden and Nursery)
(open March–December)

What Happens Here

Using colonial-style tools, such as hoes, spades, rakes, and wheelbarrows, and eighteenth-century techniques, gardeners show how plants were grown in the eighteenth century. You can also learn about eighteenth-century solutions, such as bee bottles and bell glasses, to age-old problems. The garden displays many rare and unusual varieties of heirloom vegetables as well as a collection of heirloom roses and fruits. The garden also offers items for sale, including seeds and reproduction tools.

GUNSMITH AND FOUNDRY
RECONSTRUCTED BUILDING
TICKET REQUIRED

What Happens Here

In the eighteenth century, there were two principal ways to shape metal: hammer it, which was generally the work of a smith, or cast it, which meant melting metal and pouring it into a mold. The latter was the work of a founder. The shape of the article and the material from which it was made were probably the most important factors in determining whether it would be hammered or cast. The cast items made here were usually of brass, silver, or pewter. For brass and silver, founders make molds of a sand and clay mixture that can withstand the two thousand–degree temperature of the molten metal

they then pour into it. Gunsmiths, too, cast metals in order to make parts like a trigger guard or butt plate, but they are called "smiths" because of the forge work required to make gun barrels, lock parts, and sheet metal mounts. They are masters of many trades. A finished weapon requires hammering metal into complex shapes, shaping the wooden stock, fine detail work on iron and steel, and engraving hard and soft metals.

THE PEOPLE

In 1761, David and William Geddy advertised in the *Virginia Gazette* that they were carrying on the trades of gunsmiths and founders behind the Geddy House. David and William were continuing a tradition started by their father, James Geddy Sr. In addition to gunsmithing and brass founding, the brothers were also skilled, according to their ad, as buckle makers and sword cutlers. Their brother, James Geddy Jr., later established a silversmith and jewelry business on the property, but David and William continued to operate their business behind the Geddy home.

MILLINER, MANTUA-MAKER, AND TAILOR
(Margaret Hunter Shop)
ORIGINAL BUILDING
TICKET REQUIRED

THE BUILDING

The Margaret Hunter Shop is typical of eighteenth-century commercial buildings with its gable-end facade and two-room divided interior: a large unheated storefront and a smaller counting office with a fireplace in the back.

WHAT HAPPENS HERE

The three trades at the Margaret Hunter Shop—milliners, mantua-makers, and tailors—were all in the business of fashion, which mattered then as much as now. Contrary to common belief, the milliner handled a lot more than hats. She sold a wide range of imported goods such as shirts, shifts, aprons, cloaks, hoods, muffs, ruffles, and trim for gowns. As a tradesperson, the

milliner made fashion accessories and sometimes gowns, or mantuas, though mantua making was more often a separate trade. Tailors also demonstrate their trade here, making mostly clothing for men and boys that range from working apparel to the finest suits.

THE PEOPLE

As a milliner, Margaret Hunter practiced one of the few trades commonly run by women. She did so in Williamsburg between 1771 and 1787 and was the only milliner who is known to have remained open in Williamsburg during the Revolution. Margaret first worked with her sister Jane. When Jane married in 1771, their business split: Jane opened a shop in her new home across the street, and Margaret moved to the present location.

James Slate was a tailor who arrived in Williamsburg from London in 1774.

PRINTING OFFICE AND BOOKBINDERY
RECONSTRUCTED BUILDINGS
TICKET REQUIRED

WHAT HAPPENS HERE

In the Printing Office, pressmen reproduce eighteenth-century newspapers and other printed pieces using an eighteenth-century-style printing press. You won't have any doubts why it's called a press after seeing how hard it crushes paper against inked type. Besides seeing the presses in action, you can see the leather balls that are used to "beat" ink

onto the letters, samples of the printers' work, and the cases that hold the type (the upper case holds the capital letters, the lower case holds the small letters). It takes about eighteen to twenty hours to set twenty thousand or so pieces of metal type for two pages of the *Virginia Gazette*.

Books are even more time consuming and complicated to produce than newspapers. At the Bookbindery, the pages, once received from the printer, have to be folded and then beaten with a heavy hammer to make the sheets lie flat. Then the bookbinder stitches them together with linen thread. The covers of better books are made of fine leather decorated with designs.

THE PEOPLE

Williamsburg's best-known printer of the eighteenth century was William Parks, who founded the *Virginia Gazette* in 1736. In 1766, William Rind began printing a competitive newspaper. At his death, his wife, Clementina, continued the business. In 1775, Alexander Purdie started a third newspaper. Thus, in the 1770s, three competing printers published three newspapers in Williamsburg—all called the *Virginia Gazette*.

SHOEMAKER
RECONSTRUCTED BUILDING
TICKET REQUIRED

WHAT HAPPENS HERE

Shoemaking was one of the two or three most numerous trades in colonial Williamsburg. In the eighteenth century, shoe-makers stocked ready-made shoes and also made shoes to order, at a day's wait. Following a centuries-old tradition, men's and women's shoemaking were separate pursuits. Today you can see all aspects of the eighteenth-century process for making men's shoes as shoe-makers stitch shoes and boots by hand using eighteenth-century tools and techniques.

THE PEOPLE

George Wilson advertised in the *Virginia Gazette* that he specialized in shoes and boots for gentlemen. His business must have done well since, in 1773, he encouraged two or three journeymen shoemakers to apply to him "next Door to Mr. *Greenhow*'s Store." During the 1760s and 1770s, Wilson competed with between ten and twelve other Williamsburg shoemakers.

SILVERSMITH
(The Golden Ball)
RECONSTRUCTED BUILDING
TICKET REQUIRED FOR EXHIBITION SITE BUT NOT FOR SHOP

THE BUILDING
The original building on this site was built in 1724 and survived until 1907. Jeweler and silversmith James Craig established his business here in 1765. In 1772, he began advertising his store as "The Golden Ball," a trademark commonly used by jewelers and goldsmiths. Today the Golden Ball is divided into two areas. One side of the building houses the artisans at work; a shop on the other side of the building sells silver hollowware and gold and silver jewelry. An admission ticket is required for the former but not the latter.

WHAT HAPPENS HERE
All "smiths" do some type of hammering. Silversmiths

hammer silver by hand to create jewelry, flatware such as spoons, and hollowware such as drinking vessels, bowls, and sauceboats. In the days before banks, investing in silver was a way to "store" wealth and display status. The silversmiths' work, along with other silver and gold jewelry in the style of the eighteenth century, is for sale in the store next to the workshop.

THE PEOPLE
James Craig was one of sixteen or seventeen jewelers who worked in Williamsburg during the eighteenth century. He once made a pair of earrings for Patsy Custis, the stepdaughter of George Washington. He lived and worked here with his family of five and one slave until he died in the early 1790s.

WEAVER
(Taliaferro-Cole Shop)
ORIGINAL BUILDING
TICKET REQUIRED

THE BUILDING
When Colonial Williamsburg acquired the Taliaferro-Cole Shop, the eighteenth-century building was essentially intact. A late-nineteenth-century facade and earlier additions to the rear had little impact. A

coachmaker, Charles Taliaferro, owned the building from the early 1770s to the turn of the century. In the early 1800s, Jesse Cole acquired the shop and used it as a post office and general store.

What Happens Here

Virginia colonists depended heavily on imported textiles until the Revolution, after which they had to produce much of their own cloth as well as other manufactured goods. Colonial Williamsburg weavers demonstrate the skills required. They spin fibers from materials like wool, flax, and cotton into thread or yarn, and they weave cloth on eighteenth-century-style looms. They use eighteenth-century recipes for dyes, producing an amazing array of colored fibers and cloth.

WHEELWRIGHT
(Elkanah Deane Shop)
RECONSTRUCTED BUILDING
TICKET REQUIRED

THE BUILDING

In the eighteenth century, the Elkanah Deane Shop was the site of carriage making on a large scale. Wheelwrights, blacksmiths, and harnessmakers worked together to make carts, wagons, riding chairs, and carriages.

WHAT HAPPENS HERE

Like their colonial predecessors, wheelwrights fashion hubs, spokes, and rims from wood. They then join these together into wheels that can stand up to rough roads and rougher fields. An iron tire made by a blacksmith usually circles the rim's exterior. Wheelwrights also repair eighteenth-century vehicles and construct wheelbarrows, carts, and freight wagons.

WIGMAKER
(King's Arms Barber Shop)
RECONSTRUCTED BUILDING
TICKET REQUIRED

WHAT HAPPENS HERE
Also known as a perukemaker, the wigmaker served ladies and gentlemen. Wigs were made of yak, goat, horse, or human hair. The wigmaker also made fashionable hairpieces such as curls and queues. Wigs and hair were often powdered for a more formal look. The King's Arms Barber Shop also housed, as its name implied, a barber shop and hairdresser.

THE PEOPLE
Wigmaker Edward Charlton practiced the trade in Virginia for more than half a century. His customers included Thomas Jefferson, Patrick Henry, Peyton Randolph, and other founding fathers and mothers. George Washington chose not to wear a wig.

ART MUSEUMS

Admission to the combined Art Museums of Colonial Williamsburg (De-Witt Wallace Decorative Arts Museum, Abby Aldrich Rockefeller Folk Art Museum, and Bassett Hall) is included in general admission passes, or you can buy a ticket for the museums alone. Tickets are sold in the museum gift shop but are not sold at Bassett Hall, so be sure to purchase your ticket ahead of your visit to Bassett Hall. Enter the DeWitt Wallace Decorative Arts Museum and the Abby Aldrich Rockefeller Folk Art Museum through the Public Hospital.

DEWITT WALLACE DECORATIVE ARTS MUSEUM

TOURING THE SITE
Tour on your own, though special tours and programs are available.

WHAT TO SEE HERE
This architecturally contemporary museum is home to an extensive collection of American and British antiques, including furniture, metals, ceramics, glass, paintings, prints, maps,

firearms, and textiles from the seventeenth, eighteenth, and early nineteenth centuries. The museum also hosts lectures, dramatic presentations, and musical performances in the Hennage Auditorium. A café offers light refreshments.

ABBY ALDRICH ROCKEFELLER FOLK ART MUSEUM

TOURING THE SITE
Tour on your own, though special tours and programs are available.

WHAT TO SEE HERE
Working outside the mainstream of academic art, folk artists use bold colors, simplified shapes, and imaginative surface patterns in creating a variety of paintings, carvings, furniture, metal wares, ceramics, toys, quilts, and needlework. The Folk Art Museum offers changing exhibitions of American folk art from its permanent holdings and museum loan shows.

BASSETT HALL

TOURING THE SITE
Interpreter-led tours run regularly and last about thirty minutes. While waiting for the tour, you can tour on your own a small exhibit and watch an eleven-minute video about the Rockefeller family's role in the restoration of Colonial Williamsburg's Historic Area.

WHAT TO SEE HERE
It was in this eighteenth-century frame house, located on 585 acres of gardens and rolling woodlands, that John D. Rockefeller Jr. and his wife, Abby Aldrich Rockefeller, made their home during the early restoration of the Historic Area, a restoration they financed. Today the house looks much as it did in the 1930s and 1940s when the Rockefellers restored and furnished it to be a comfortable family home.

GARDENS

Colonial Williamsburg's Historic Area gardens range from the formal splendor of the Governor's Palace gardens to the utilitarian kitchen garden at Wetherburn's Tavern. Ongoing research continues to provide a better understanding of eighteenth-century Williamsburg gardens so that they more fully reflect the variety of lifestyles in the city. You are welcome to walk through the gardens at your leisure. Even gardens attached to private residences are open to the public. Note, however, that four of the sites require a ticket to enjoy the garden: the James Geddy House, Governor's Palace, Benjamin Powell House, and George Wythe House. Listed below are some of the most popular gardens.

DR. BARRAUD HOUSE
Archaeological investigations uncovered some of the best-preserved marl walks in Williamsburg, giving a clear indication of the garden's original layout.

BASSETT HALL
The gardens have been re-created as they were when the house served as the Williamsburg home of Mr. and Mrs. John D. Rockefeller Jr. in the 1940s. A boxwood vista borders the west side of large flowerbeds that are planted with bulbs in the spring and mums in the fall.

JOHN BLAIR HOUSE
This garden, reminiscent of the "physick" gardens popular in the seventeenth century, is comprised of parterres planted with herbs used by the colonists primarily for their scent.

BRACKEN TENEMENT
The garden design has been kept simple with a small parterre immediately to the rear of the house. Yaupon holly has been used in three different ways here—as enclosing hedge, as topiary accents, and in a natural screen.

BRYAN HOUSE

An arbor covered with native honeysuckle and American wisteria offers a splendid view of the carefully trimmed boxwood parterres. This garden was based on garden patterns depicted on Claude Joseph Sauthier's maps of North Carolina towns of about 1769.

CHRISTIANA CAMPBELL'S TAVERN

The beautiful geometric garden beside the tavern consists of nine planting beds with a tiered topiary yaupon holly in the central circle. Flowering dogwoods, oak-leaf hydrangeas, red chokeberries, and eastern red cedars create seasonal interest.

ELIZABETH CARLOS HOUSE

The pleasure garden is a typical four-square pattern employing a well house as focal point. A carefully trimmed hedge of yaupon holly surrounds four parterres planted with heirloom flowers.

COKE-GARRETT HOUSE

Stately evergreens, nut trees, and old boxwood enclose the area behind the house and lead down a grassy ramp to a flower border on the lower garden level.

COLONIAL GARDEN AND NURSERY

Gardeners are on-site to discuss eighteenth-century horticulture. The garden displays many rare and unusual varieties of heirloom vegetables as well as a collection of heirloom roses and fruits. The garden also offers items for sale, including seeds and reproduction tools.

ALEXANDER CRAIG HOUSE

Gardens and outbuildings were mentioned in the recorded deeds for this original house. Today the pleasure garden provides an attractive foreground to the orchard's fruit trees, pleached arbors, and the original brickbat paths.

CUSTIS TENEMENT

The parterre garden, partially enclosed by English boxwood,

features formal paths made of crushed shell and brick. The seasonal flower beds are edged with germander.

THOMAS EVERARD HOUSE

The pleasure garden behind the house is filled with mature English boxwood. The oldest were likely planted about 1850.

JAMES GEDDY HOUSE
TICKET REQUIRED

Among the items listed in the inventory made at the time of James Geddy Sr.'s death in 1744 were three "potting pots," one "Garden Water pot," and four "Water pales." As tradespeople, the Geddys were probably not doing extensive gardening, but the presence of garden implements suggests some effort, most likely the cultivation of vegetables and herbs.

GOVERNOR'S PALACE
TICKET REQUIRED

The complex of gardens, spread over ten acres, resembles English country estates during the reign of King William III and Queen Mary II. The Bodleian Plate, a copperplate found in 1929, shows the property in detail and helped landscape architect Arthur Shurcliff re-create the Palace gardens.

The garden's original features include the falling gardens (terraces), the canal, and the ice mount.

ORLANDO JONES HOUSE

The presence of a garden is based on a 1745 advertisement in the *Virginia Gazette*. The garden features boxwood topiary, a hornbeam aerial hedge, and seasonal flower beds.

KING'S ARMS TAVERN

An arbor provides deep shade for a twenty-first-century

outdoor dining area. In the kitchen garden, the crosswalks meet at a round bed that is edged on the outside with cordoned apple trees.

David MORTON HOUSE

The positioning of the house and outbuildings, as shown on a 1782 map and substantiated by archaeological excavations, was the determining factor in re-creating this formal garden. An arbor covered with muscadine grapes serves as a backdrop for the covered well and pump.

PALMER HOUSE

Tucked beside this home is a symmetrical pleasure garden designed around a central sundial. Oyster-shell pathways define four circular beds planted with perennial bulbs and shade-loving perennials. Surrounded by boxwood hedges, the garden offers passersby a secluded spot.

PASTEUR & GALT APOTHECARY SHOP

The "simples" seen in the garden behind the shop are representative of medicinal herbs used in the colony.

Benjamin POWELL HOUSE
TICKET REQUIRED

The Powell garden illustrates the axial arrangement of garden spaces typical of colonial site development. Behind the small pleasure garden and separated by the work yard is a kitchen garden featuring vegetables, fruits, and herbs in season.

PRENTIS HOUSE

The pleasure garden, behind the service yard, has been designed with six parterres edged in yaupon holly. The small orchard near the back street is balanced by the stable and paddock at the rear of the site.

ALEXANDER PURDIE HOUSE

The pleasure garden features a simple four-square design with sixteen identically sheared yaupon topiaries within four turf panels defined by brick crosswalks. Plants of seasonal interest include shadblow trees, pomegranates, and oakleaf hydrangeas.

GEORGE REID HOUSE

The original well is located in the service yard behind this original house. Directly behind the service yard is a kitchen garden featuring heirloom flowers, vegetables, and herbs. Next, an orchard with heirloom fruit trees leads to the paddock with a stable.

TALIAFERRO-COLE HOUSE

Thomas Crease, a professional

gardener in eighteenth-century Williamsburg, lived on this site for a total of thirty-five years. The topography of the site is largely unchanged from his time.

WETHERBURN'S TAVERN

Behind the kitchen and adjacent outbuildings is a simple square kitchen garden. The contents of a well on the site, examined during archaeological investigations, were found to include the stones, seeds, and other remains of common fruits and vegetables.

GEORGE WYTHE HOUSE
TICKET REQUIRED

Surviving letters reveal that Wythe gave fruit from his garden to Thomas Jefferson. Today, a kitchen garden, an orchard, and the service yard with outbuildings flank each side of the pleasure garden. A pleached American hornbeam arbor terminates the main garden path.

Produce from the gardens is used in presentations by the Foodways staff or is allowed to go to seed so that gardeners can preserve the heirloom varieties.

RARE BREEDS

Animals were very much a part of eighteenth-century life in Virginia. Colonial Williamsburg's Rare Breeds program presents animals that were or could have been present here then and that might very well not be present at all today were it not for preservation efforts like those of the Foundation. You'll find animals, both rare breeds and not, throughout the Historic Area—on the streets, in open pastures, and on the grounds of some exhibition sites. Please don't feed or pet them.

LEICESTER LONGWOOL SHEEP

Leicester (pronounced "lester") Longwools originated in Britain and were pioneers in America, Australia, New Zealand, and other British colonies. Today they are quite rare. These sheep have long, healthy, lustrous coats that fall in ringlets. Their wool is sold to hand spinners, weavers, felters, and doll makers for hair and beards. The original herd of Colonial Williamsburg's Leicester Longwool sheep came from Tasmania, but now the sheep are bred here. You can see the new lambs among the flock in the spring. You can also sometimes see shearing being done by hand in the spring.

AMERICAN CREAM DRAFT HORSES

The only modern breed in the program also is the rarest—just over five hundred still exist in North America. Breed characteristics include a medium cream–colored coat, pink skin, amber eyes, a long white mane and tail, and white markings. These horses mature late at five years old and have an excellent temperament. Currently, the Foundation has only one young gelding.

CANADIAN HORSES

Canadian horses were developed from horses sent from France to Quebec between 1665 and 1670. Canadians were used for farm work, transport, riding, and racing.

They are solid and well muscled with well-arched necks set high on long sloping shoulders. Canadians are primarily black or reddish brown with full manes and tails. They are energetic without being nervous and are adaptable for a variety of riding and driving disciplines. Currently, the Foundation has only one gelding. You may see him being ridden by costumed interpreters as well as pulling wagons and carriages.

AMERICAN MILKING RED DEVON COWS
Diversity is the trademark of this breed. Their milk contains a high butterfat content, prized

in the eighteenth century for butter and cheese production. They also provide quality meat, are very intelligent, and are good work animals. Today their milk is used occasionally in the Historic Area Foodways program. Descended from the Red Devon breed native to Devonshire, England, American Milking Devons now are bred here.

MILKING SHORTHORN AND RANDALL OXEN
The trucks, tractors, and bulldozers of the eighteenth century, oxen are cattle trained to work. Milking Shorthorns originated in England, can be red or white, and are used for milk, meat, and work. Randalls were bred in Vermont by a family of the same name. They are also called Linebacks because of the white line that runs down their backs. Oxen can be found working throughout the Historic Area, particularly at Great Hopes Plantation.

DOMINIQUE CHICKENS

One of the first breeds of chickens developed in America, these are small to medium in size and have very hardy constitutions. Their heavy plumage protects them from cold winters.

NANKIN BANTAM CHICKENS

Called yellow bantams in colonial times, these are handsome birds with rose combs setting off their gold body color and shiny black main tail feathers.

ENGLISH GAME FOWL

Originally bred for cockfighting, these are distinguished by their strength, agility, and aggressiveness. They lost popularity after cockfighting was banned, but they produce high-quality meat and eggs.

Not all the animals you'll see in the Historic Area are rare breeds, though all have connections to colonial times. Ossabaw Island pigs, for example, were left on one of Georgia's barrier islands by Spanish explorers in the sixteenth century. These dark-colored, trim-looking animals actually provide very fatty meat.

MUSIC

Music was an important part of eighteenth-century life. Today you can find original and authentic period instruments and music throughout the Historic Area.

Popular instruments in the eighteenth century included the spinet, harpsichord, piano, guitar, violin, French horn, flute, fife, oboe, recorder, organ, and banjo. Both males and females, free and enslaved played musical instruments. Check "This Week" for scheduled musical programs during the day and evening. You will also encounter music and musical instruments as you tour various buildings and in Revolutionary City. In the historic dining taverns, balladeers provide musical entertainment, including many eighteenth-century songs.

FIFES AND DRUMS

A Colonial Williamsburg icon, the Fifes and Drums preserve the eighteenth-century tradition of military music.

With the onset of war in 1775, Virginia not only enlisted soldiers and stockpiled arms but also trained fifers and drummers to work with soldiers in the field. Fifes and drums served as signal instruments for the infantry, relaying the commander's orders to soldiers in camp and on the field of battle. The steady rhythm and spirited tunes of the fifers and drummers also kept soldiers' minds off the tedium of marching.

The Colonial Williamsburg Fifes and Drums carry forward the tradition of military music, giving hundreds of performances a year, both in the Historic Area and elsewhere. In the eighteenth century, fifers and drummers tended to be boys aged ten to eighteen. Today's fifers and drummers are also aged ten to eighteen but include girls as well as boys. See "This Week" for scheduled performances of the Colonial Williamsburg Fifes and Drums.

NIGHTLIFE

Singing and dancing, theater and movies, witches and ghosts. Colonial Williamsburg's programs don't end with nightfall. Separate tickets are required for most evening programs and seating is limited, so book early.

What programs you might see depends on when you visit. You might want to learn the "new" dance steps at the candlelit Capitol or take in an elegant evening of chamber music at the Palace. Join in songs and dances adapted by the eighteenth-century African-American community from West African traditions. Explore colonial trades sites by "lanthorn" light. Become a member of a court determining whether a Virginia officer who abandoned his post in the face of a British attack was a coward or traitor or weigh the evidence at a witch trial. Enjoy an eighteenth-century play, as Thomas Jefferson did, or harpsichord music from Peter Pelham, the eighteenth-century organist of Bruton Parish Church. Enlist in the Continental army or listen as free and enslaved African Americans reflect on lessons learned through stories told by their elders. Listen to tales of mystery and the unexplained or bring the entire family to hear storytellers share centuries-old legends.

In Merchants Square, adjacent to the Historic Area, the Kimball Theatre is home to current films as well as live performances. On any given day, you might see an interpreter portraying Patrick Henry or a jazz ensemble from the College of William and Mary or an eighteenth-century "Grand Medley of Entertainments."

Check "This Week" to see what is offered during the time of your visit. To purchase tickets or for more information, go to any ticket sales location or call 1-800-HISTORY (447-8679).

HIGHLIGHTS FOR FIRST-TIME GUESTS

Your own interests may lead you to particular sites, but, if this is your first visit or your first visit in a long time and you aren't sure where to go, we recommend the following sites and programs. They will also give you a well-rounded view of colonial Williamsburg:

- Revolutionary City
- Capitol
- Courthouse
- Governor's Palace
- Magazine
- Peyton Randolph House
- Blacksmith
- Printing Office and Book-bindery
- Art Museums of Colonial Williamsburg

HIGHLIGHTS FOR FAMILIES

The following are some options that are particularly interesting to children:

- Costume Rentals. Available at Williamsburg Revolutions at the Visitor Center and seasonally at the outdoor booths on Market Square.
- Gateway Building and Kid's Corner
- Children's Orientation Walk. Meet at the Gateway Building for this thirty-minute tour. See "This Week" for times.
- Carriage Rides. Space is limited, so purchase tickets early.
- Get Revved! A program for kids to get the most out of the Revolutionary City program.
- Stocks and Pillory, beside the Courthouse
- Magazine
- Palace Maze and Cellar
- Public Gaol
- James Geddy House and Gunsmith and Foundry
- Great Hopes Plantation
- Blacksmith
- Colonial Garden
- Milliner, Mantua-maker, and Tailor
- Printing Office and Book-bindery
- Silversmith
- Animals
- Art Museums of Colonial Williamsburg. Printed family guides are available, as is a special audio tour for teens.
- Retail Stores: Post Office, Tarpley's Store, Everything Williamsburg
- Dining: Raleigh Tavern Bakery, Chowning's Tavern
- Evening Programs: "A Grand Medley of Entertainments," "Listen My Children," "African-American Music," and "Papa Said, Mama Said." Additional ticket required.

SPECIAL EVENTS

Whether it's Fourth of July fireworks or film festivals at the Kimball Theatre, Colonial Williamsburg features special events and programs throughout the year.

WORKING WOOD IN THE EIGHTEENTH CENTURY

This multi-day January conference, cosponsored with *Fine Woodworking* magazine, offers lectures and workshops on various woodworking topics. Colonial Williamsburg tradespeople, curators, and conservators as well as other specialists discuss and demonstrate various styles and techniques related to the year's theme.

BLACK HISTORY MONTH

In February, Colonial Williamsburg offers dramatic interpretive programs that bring to life stories of the African-American struggle for freedom and liberty during the eighteenth century.

ANTIQUES FORUM

This February conference explores various aspects of the decorative arts, including early American furniture, silver, ceramics, textiles, paintings, and buildings. Widely known experts investigate these exquisite objects. Curators, collectors, and historians present their latest findings in a series of illustrated and video-assisted workshops and presentations.

WOMEN'S HISTORY MONTH

In March, Colonial Williamsburg scenes, tours, programs, and special presentations explore the various roles that our foremothers filled in birthing a nation.

GARDEN SYMPOSIUM

At this spring conference, cosponsored with the American Horticultural Society, Colonial Williamsburg garden experts and other professionals offer advice on many aspects of gardening including design concepts, gardening techniques, and plant selection.

MEMORIAL DAY

This annual commemorative program honors those who died in service to our country. Wreaths are placed at several sites where the remains of military dead from three centuries rest. Prayers, cannon and musket fire, and music of the Fifes and Drums are all incorporated.

MASONIC PROCESSIONS AND SERVICES

On June 24 and December 27, the feast days of St. John the Baptist and St. John the Evangelist, respectively, were celebrated annually by the Masonic Lodge of eighteenth-century Williamsburg. Lodge members processed from the lodge to the church to hear a sermon preached for their benefit by the chaplain of the Lodge. Colonial Williamsburg's modern-day re-enactments include costumed interpreters, current members of Williamsburg Lodge No. 6, and guests who are Masons who choose to participate.

UNDER THE REDCOAT

In June, witness the arrival of the British army as they seize Williamsburg, raise the British flag over the Capitol, and commence occupation of the town. Learn how life in eighteenth-century Williamsburg changed under British rule.

INDEPENDENCE DAY

Hear a reading of the Declaration of Independence and performances from Colonial Williamsburg's Fifes and Drums. Fireworks fill the sky after sundown.

STORYTELLING CONCERTS

Professional storytellers spin their yarns during a series of concerts over the third weekend in September.

PRELUDE TO VICTORY

In October, meet General Washington and his army on their way to lay siege to Yorktown in what proves to be the decisive battle of the American Revolution. Join other townspeople and offer encouragement as the army displays its proficiency in firing demonstrations. General Washington and his officers address the battalion concerning the upcoming siege.

VETERANS DAY

Colonial Williamsburg honors America's veterans with a procession down Duke of Gloucester Street. The parade culminates in a public ceremony with militia and cannon crew firing volleys in recognition of those who serve. Hear Colonial Williamsburg's Fifes and Drums alongside voices from past and present.

CHRISTMAS

Truth be told, Christmas in colonial times bore little resemblance to today's celebrations. It was primarily a religious holiday, though there was plenty of celebrating. Today, Williamsburg is rightly famed for its creative use of fresh greens and fruits as decorations, and millions have visited to admire them. A highlight of the season today is Grand Illumination, when candles twinkle in the windows, fatwood crackles in street-side cressets, and fireworks explode overhead.

Grand Illumination takes place ten days after Thanksgiving, which is the Sunday of the first full weekend in December. Between Thanksgiving and the first week of January, Colonial Williamsburg offers hundreds of holiday events, including dancing, music, and the traditional firing of the Christmas guns.

SHOPPING

HISTORIC AREA SHOPS

The shops in the Historic Area have some truly unique items. Some of the shops, like the Golden Ball, the Colonial Nursery, and the Post Office, carry specific types of items. Other shops, like the John Greenhow Store, the Market Square stands, and Tarpley's Store, stock a wider selection of goods, with offerings often overlapping but each shop reflecting its colonial origins.

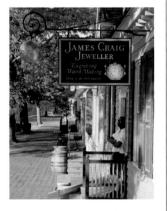

using eighteenth-century tools and techniques, including richly handcrafted leather goods, iron hardware, reproduction pottery, furniture, and baskets.

THE GOLDEN BALL
(Jeweler)

Reproductions of precious gemstone rings, earrings, pendants, and charms in sterling silver and 14-karat gold. You'll also find beautifully crafted brass, pewter hollowware, and one-of-a-kind sterling pieces created by Colonial Williamsburg's silversmith.

PRENTIS STORE
ORIGINAL BUILDING

Features one-of-a-kind items, handmade by Colonial Williamsburg's skilled tradespeople

JOHN GREENHOW STORE

Wrought iron, willow baskets, fine imported porcelain, floorcloths, fabrics, cooper's items, tinware, craftsmen's tools, and other goods similar to those sold by Mr. Greenhow in the eighteenth century.

COLONIAL GARDEN AND NURSERY

Gardening items including heirloom seeds and plants, herbs, flowers, seasonal greens, wreaths, eighteenth-century clay flower pots, and bird bottles.

MARY DICKINSON STORE

Eighteenth-century fashion in the best of taste: petticoats, short gowns, cloaks, mitts, caps, and beautifully decorated straw hats—all made in Williamsburg. Jewelry and ladies' toiletries as well.

MARKET SQUARE STANDS

An open-air market selling toys, hats, pottery, and baskets. Also, rentals of eighteenth-century costumes for boys and girls and auctions of new goods from Historic Area stores.

POST OFFICE

Reproduction prints, maps, leather-bound books, stationery, quill pens, ink, inkwells, and sealing wax. Letters and postcards hand-canceled with reproduction eighteenth-century Williamsburg postmark. Stamps available.

TARPLEY'S STORE

Toys, games, candies, soaps, period clothing, hats, and jewelry.

MERCHANTS SQUARE SHOPS

Located adjacent to the Historic Area, near the Wren Building of the College of William and Mary, is Merchants Square. This retail village was America's first shopping center and remains a national landmark. Enjoy more than forty specialty shops and dining establishments, including the following Colonial Williamsburg stores.

WILLIAMSBURG AT HOME

Flagship store of Williamsburg-brand home furnishings and accessories including furniture, bedding, rugs, light fixtures, prints, fabrics, and decorative accessories.

WILLIAMSBURG CELEBRATIONS

Byers' Choice®, Department 56, and other classic Williamsburg-brand collectibles. A full assortment of holiday decorations, seasonal floral arrangements, and garden accessories.

WILLIAMSBURG CRAFT HOUSE

Choose from the full line of Williamsburg-brand dinnerware, flatware, glassware, pewter, silver, delft, fine ceramic giftware, folk art, and jewelry. An exclusive selection of personalized gifts, including engraving.

EVERYTHING WILLIAMSBURG

From T-shirts to toys, a broad selection of exclusive Colonial Williamsburg souvenirs.

OTHER SHOPPING

Shopping opportunities are also available at the gift shops in Colonial Williamsburg hotels, the Museum Store in the Art Museums of Colonial Williamsburg, the pro shops at the golf courses, and the boutique at the Spa of Colonial Williamsburg. The Visitor Center houses the following sizable establishments.

WILLIAMSBURG BOOKSELLERS

A wide selection of books, CDs, and DVDs for all ages on countless colonial topics.

WILLIAMSBURG REVOLUTIONS

Games, toys, gifts, food, and Colonial Williamsburg logo apparel, as well as costume rentals.

GOLF

The Golden Horseshoe Golf Club, located just beyond the Williamsburg Inn and across the street from the Williamsburg Lodge, includes two eighteen-hole championship courses and one nine-hole executive-length course surrounded by Audubon sanctuaries. The Golden Horseshoe earned a listing among the "Top 75 Golf Resorts Around the World" by Condé Nast Traveler and the Gold and Green Courses are rated four and a half stars by Golf Digest. Open seven days a week, 365 days a year, 7 a.m.–6 p.m. To book your tee time, call (757) 220-7696 or 1-800-648-6653.

GOLD COURSE

Opened in 1963 and the work of Robert Trent Jones Sr., who called it his "finest design," this is one of the best examples of traditional golf course architecture in the world.

> 18 holes
> Yardage: 6,817
> Par: 71

GREEN COURSE

Designed by Rees Jones, Robert Trent Jones Sr.'s son, and opened in 1991, this layout is carved from the same terrain but is simultaneously longer and more forgiving.

> 18 holes
> Yardage: 7,120
> Par: 72

SPOTSWOOD COURSE

This is the elder Jones's 1963 update of the Williamsburg Inn's original 1947 nine-hole course.

> 9 holes
> Yardage: 3,745
> Par: 31

SPA

From the botanicals used in the seventeenth century to the revolutionary advancements of the twenty-first century, the therapies at the Spa of Colonial Williamsburg have withstood the test of time.

Among the featured options at the Spa are the Cleansing Hot Stones Spa Experience (inspired by seventeenth-century treatments), the Colonial Herbal Spa Experience (eighteenth century), the Root and Herbal Spa Experience (nineteenth century), the Williamsburg Water Cures Spa Experience (twentieth century), and the Skin Rejuvenation Spa Experience (twenty-first cen-

tury). Spa services include massages, body treatments, baths, professional skin care, and the conservatory salon. A comprehensive fitness studio, including indoor and outdoor pools, is also available at the spa.

Located between the Williamsburg Inn and Williamsburg Lodge. Reservations are highly recommended. Call 1-800-688-6479, (757) 220-7720, or in-house extension 7720.

RESTAURANTS

In and around the Historic Area, you can choose from among historic dining taverns that carry on eighteenth-century traditions, snack concessions, and a range of contemporary restaurants.

HISTORIC AREA DINING

In the eighteenth century, Williamsburg's taverns provided lodgings for travelers as well as serving as places to gather for meals, conversation, and entertainment. Today, Colonial Williamsburg's historic dining taverns carry on these traditions by providing a relaxed and comfortable setting for diners to experience some of the flavor of the past—through atmosphere, entertainments, and food. Taverns operate seasonally, so check what's open.

TAVERNS

For lunch, a quick option, and a very enjoyable choice in pleasant weather, is the outdoor Garden Bar behind Chowning's Tavern. The counter service there offers soups, salads, sandwiches, burgers, and barbecue. Seating is picnic-table style under a grape arbor. Chowning's Tavern itself offers similar food choices but with table service in an indoor dining room. Chowning's Tavern utilizes common seating, with most tables seating four to six.

For a more leisurely lunch, consider Shields Tavern, the King's Arms Tavern, or Christiana Campbell's Tavern. These menus are more diverse. Shields specializes in "southern comfort food." The King's Arms serves traditional fare including its trademark peanut soup. Christiana Campbell's features seafood items, with crab cakes being a specialty. While all of the taverns welcome all guests and none require special dress, the King's Arms and Christiana Campbell's are your best bets for a more intimate dinner whereas Shields has a more open atmosphere. All of the taverns offer children's menu options.

All four taverns have full bars and offer specialty drinks, but only Chowning's hosts Gambols. From 5 p.m., enjoy casual fare and a variety of

lively entertainment, such as a magician, eighteenth-century games, and sing-alongs. The other three taverns feature balladeers at night.

Dinner reservations are required at Shields, King's Arms, and Christiana Campbell's. Make reservations at the Visitor Center or by calling 1-800-TAVERNS (828-3767) or (757) 229-2141.

LIGHT LUNCHES, SNACKS, AND TREATS
The Raleigh Tavern Bakery (behind the Raleigh Tavern) offers cookies, muffins, rolls, and other pastries as well as ham biscuits and sandwiches and hot and cold drinks. While some items are familiar staples, others offer a taste of days gone by. Seating is available in the bakery courtyard and in the garden behind the bakery.

For a quick snack, stop by Chowning's Cider Stand (next to Chowning's Tavern), Mr. Shields Storehouse (behind Shields Tavern), or McKenzie Apothecary. All are seasonal, small counter-service concessions offering drinks and light refreshments.

Souvenir mugs and refills to go are available at Mr. Shields Storehouse, Chowning's Cider Stand, Chowning's Garden Bar, McKenzie Apothecary, the Raleigh Tavern Bakery, and the Visitor Center Café.

OTHER COLONIAL WILLIAMSBURG DINING
At the elegant Williamsburg Inn, the Regency Room is renowned for its culinary classics

and seasonal dishes, including a dry-aged Angus fillet of beef, sweet lobster bisque, and citrus-glazed scallops with herbed prawns. It also features an award-winning wine list and delicious desserts. Appropriate dress is required. Resort casual during the day. Jackets are required and no denim is permitted for dinner and Sunday brunch. For a more casual dining experience at the

Inn, the Terrace Room offers sandwiches and entrées including a Kobe beef burger, braised Angus short ribs, and three-cheese pasta. Lighter fare such as chicken Cobb and Spa salads are also available. The Restoration Bar is perfect for cocktails and nightcaps.

The Williamsburg Lodge Restaurant serves American cuisine with contemporary southern and Chesapeake influences. The Friday night seafood buffet is very popular. A children's menu is available.

At the Lodge lobby lounge and bar light fare available includes burgers and paninis.

Huzzah! is on the Visitor Center promenade and adjacent to the Williamsburg Woodlands Hotel & Suites. This family eatery offers everyday favorites such as house-made soups, oversized burgers, wraps, pasta, and hand-tossed pizza. Children's menu available.

Each of the Golden Horseshoe Golf Courses features a clubhouse where you can enjoy a meal and a view. At both the Gold Course Clubhouse Grill and Green Course Clubhouse Grill, menu items include sandwiches, soups, salads, and desserts. Outdoor dining is available seasonally.

In the Visitor Center, the Visitor Center Café offers snacks, drinks, and sandwiches.

The Museum Café in the DeWitt Wallace Decorative Arts Museum includes sandwiches, salads, and soups plus tea, coffee, and wine.

Dinner reservations are recommended at Colonial Williamsburg restaurants. Lunch reservations are recommended for the Regency Room. Make reservations at the Visitor Center or call 1-800-TAVERNS (828-3767) or (757) 229-2141.

MERCHANTS SQUARE DINING

Merchants Square offers a range of dining options from ice cream, pizza, and sandwiches to AAA four-diamond full-service restaurants.

Hotels

When John D. Rockefeller Jr. undertook to restore Williamsburg in the 1930s, he wanted guests to have a place to stay nearby. The initial result was the Williamsburg Inn. Colonial Williamsburg has since built or restored additional lodging options to accommodate its guests.

A destination in itself, the Williamsburg Inn is one of the world's great luxury hotels: a home away from home for royalty (twice hosting Queen Elizabeth II), heads of state, celebrities, and guests from around the globe. Meticulous renovations retained the graceful elegance of the Inn while updating every aspect of its

interior. Guest rooms average a generous five hundred square feet with luxurious marble bathrooms, English Regency-style furnishings, and comfortable seating areas. The hotel offers an outdoor pool, tennis courts, croquet, and lawn bowling.

The Providence Hall Guesthouses offer the resort pleasures of the Williamsburg Inn set within the privacy and serenity of a wooded area with

pond and waterfowl. The Providence Hall Guesthouses are located a short walk from the main Williamsburg Inn building. Rooms are appointed with luxurious king-size beds and queen-size sleeper sofas.

The Williamsburg Lodge offers leisure and conference guests a helping of southern hospitality with superb service. A total of eight buildings are connected by sheltered, brick-paved walkways. Suites are available. Swimming, tennis, croquet, and lawn bowling are available at the nearby Williamsburg Inn.

A rare way to experience the Historic Area, the Colonial Houses–Historic Lodging offer twenty-six period accommodations right in the Historic Area. Accommodations range in size from one room in a tavern to a sixteen–room house. Scattered throughout the Historic Area, these lodgings are furnished with authentic period reproductions and antiques, and some have wood-burning fireplaces, canopy beds, and sitting rooms. All include modern amenities.

Adjacent to Colonial Williamsburg's Visitor Center, the moderately priced Williamsburg Woodlands Hotel & Suites is a family haven with recreational choices that include

miniature golf, shuffleboard, table tennis, bike rentals, and swimming. A continental breakfast buffet is included in the room rate. Rooms feature two full-size beds, a sitting area with desk, and a comfortable lounge chair (convertible to a single bed). Suites offer a lounging room with a queen sofa bed, desk, and convenience counter with a small refrigerator, microwave, sink, and coffeemaker, plus a separate master bedroom with a king-size bed and second television. Walk or shuttle to the Historic Area.

The most economical of Colonial Williamsburg's hotels, the Governor's Inn offers comfortable accommodations, an outdoor swimming pool, free

use of the recreational facilities of the nearby Williamsburg Woodlands Hotel & Suites, and a continental breakfast included in the room rate. The Governor's Inn is located two blocks from Merchants Square and three blocks from the Historic Area. Open seasonally.

THE HISTORIC TRIANGLE

Williamsburg is one point in America's Historic Triangle. The other two are Jamestown and Yorktown. Linked by the scenic twenty-three-mile Colonial Parkway, Jamestown, Williamsburg, and Yorktown were crucial stops on our nation's journey from the first English settlement to the decisive victory that secured liberty and independence.

In 1607, three ships landed at Cape Henry, Virginia. They soon proceeded up a river to establish the first permanent English settlement in America. To honor the king who sent them, the explorers named the river the James, and the settlement Jamestown.

In 1699, the capital of the Virginia Colony moved to Williamsburg. It was here that the idea of a free and independent country began.

The last great engagement of the American Revolution was the Battle of Yorktown. In 1781, the Continental army defeated the British redcoats, fulfilling the promise of the Declaration of Independence.

JAMESTOWN

Historic Jamestowne encompasses the island where the settlers first landed. You can see where archaeologists excavated the 1607 James Fort and, at the Nathalie P. and Alan M. Voorhees Archaearium, examine artifacts the archaeologists uncovered. You can take a walk in the New Towne area along the James River, visit the reconstructed seventeenth-century Memorial Church, and watch costumed glassblowers demonstrate their trade. The National Park Service, Preservation Virginia, and Colonial Williamsburg jointly administer Historic Jamestowne.

At Jamestown Settlement, just off the island, you can board replicas of the original ships to experience what seventeenth-century explorers endured on their passage to the New World. You can explore the world of Pocahontas and the Powhatan Indians in a re-created Indian village and that of the colonists in a re-created fort. Indoor galleries trace Jamestown's beginnings in England through the first century of the colony and describe the cultures of the Powhatan Indians, Europeans, and Africans who converged in seventeenth-century Virginia. Jamestown Settlement is administered by the Commonwealth of Virginia.

YORKTOWN

At the Yorktown Battlefield Visitor Center, you can see a film about the siege of Yorktown and you can view George Washington's military tents and artifacts from the siege. Out-side, you can walk around the battlefield or take a seven-mile self-guided driving tour along American and French siege lines and see where the surrender took place. In the town of Yorktown, you can visit, among other historic buildings, the home of Thomas Nelson Jr., a signer of the Declaration of Independence. The National Park Service administers Yorktown Battlefield.

On the other side of Yorktown, at the Yorktown Victory Center, there are galleries on the Declaration of Independence, the impact of the war on ordinary men and women, the roles of different nationalities at the siege of Yorktown, and British ships lost in the river during the siege. Outdoors, you can visit a re-created Continental army encampment, where interpreters describe and depict the daily life of soldiers, and a re-created 1780s farm. The Yorktown Victory Center is run by the Commonwealth of Virginia.

FREQUENTLY ASKED QUESTIONS

Why do I need a ticket?
Your admission pass gives you access to historic homes and buildings, other exhibition sites, and Revolutionary City. See how families lived, how trades were practiced, where laws were made, and how colonists played, all with the guidance of knowledgeable costumed interpreters.

Where should I start?
Begin your visit at the Visitor Center with ample parking, restrooms, and information about current programs, exhibitions, and activities. Purchase your tickets and get a current copy of "This Week," the weekly guide to schedules and programs. From here, it's a quarter-mile walk across the pedestrian bridge to the Historic Area. Read the time line plaques along the bridge and prepare yourself for your transitions to and from the eighteenth century.

When can I visit?
Colonial Williamsburg is open 365 days a year. Go to www
.history.org/visit/planyourvisit/
schedule for seasonal hours of specific sites.

Which Historic Area buildings may I enter?
A site with a flag at its entrance is open. Historic Area retail shops do not require admission tickets but interpretive sites do. Not all colonial buildings are open to the public; some are privately occupied by employees of Colonial Williamsburg and their families, some hold administrative offices, and some are used for storage. Pick up a free copy of Colonial Williamsburg's weekly program guide, "This Week," at the Visitor Center or any ticket sales location. In it, you'll find a map showing which exhibition sites are open and a daily listing of programs.

Are the buildings in the Historic Area the original eighteenth-century structures?
There are nearly ninety original buildings. These include prominent structures like the Courthouse, the Magazine, and the George Wythe House as well as simpler shops, offices, and outbuildings. All of the buildings required some amount of restoration when Colonial Williamsburg acquired them. Brick structures weathered the years well, but some buildings required, for example, new framing timbers, weatherboarding, roofing, or trim. Original material was preserved whenever

possible, but some modern materials were also incorporated. On the flip side, many of the "reconstructed" buildings incorporate a great deal of the original fabric of the building.

How are buildings reconstructed?
Most of the reconstructed buildings in the Historic Area were built on their original brick foundations, which, in some cases, were revealed by archaeological digs. To reconstruct buildings, Colonial Williamsburg's architects and archaeologists draw on a variety of evidence, including what's uncovered at the site and in documents (wills, deeds, journals, early drawings, etc.) as well as a general understanding of colonial building technology and design. The reconstruction of two of the most prominent buildings, the Governor's Palace and the Capitol, relied heavily on a detailed engraving from about 1740 called the Bodleian Plate. Jefferson's sketches of his plan to remodel the Palace assisted greatly in its interior reconstruction.

How long does it take to tour the Historic Area?
The Historic Area is quite large—one mile long and half a mile wide. Over forty exhibition sites and museums, various places to shop and dine,

and numerous programs offer guests a variety of ways to relive the Revolutionary War period. Most guests find that a day is not enough, but a day can give you a sampling of the Historic Area if you start early and plan ahead. Depending on your interests or focus, you can enjoy a fuller experience in two or more days.

How much time should I plan to spend at each site?
That will vary depending on what the site offers and your interest level in the site. In general, the sites with interpreter-led tours last about thirty minutes, but sometimes you may want to linger, especially at sites with additional grounds. The Governor's Palace is the most extensive Historic Area site; you could spend hours touring the building and exploring the grounds. Also, consider that you may spend some time waiting your turn to enter a site. At the Historic Trades shops, you could be mesmerized by a tradesperson or want to watch an entire process for thirty minutes or more. Scheduled programs at various sites can last from fifteen to sixty minutes (see "This Week"). Also, the Art Museums of Colonial Williamsburg could easily fill a few hours.

What happens during bad weather?

Outdoor programs are presented weather permitting. Building tours continue during inclement weather, and the Art Museums of Colonial Williamsburg are open daily.

Where can I rent colonial costumes?

Children's costume rentals are available daily in the Visitor Center's Costume Rental Center and seasonally at the booths on Market Square.

How can I take a carriage ride?

Tickets are sold on the day of the ride at all Colonial Williamsburg ticket locations. Availability is limited and tickets are sold on a first-come, first-served basis, so purchase your ticket early in the morning. Reservations are not taken in advance due to the unpredictable nature of the weather.

Why are there horse droppings on the streets?

The horses that carry interpreters and pull carriages and wagons throughout the Historic Area do leave things behind. The livestock staff cleans up after the horses regularly, but watch your step in the meantime.

On which tours may I bring babies and young children (and strollers)?

Babies and young children are welcome but we ask that, out of consideration for others, crying children be taken out of the building or away from the program. Due to the fragile nature of furnishings and interiors, strollers are not permitted in Historic Area buildings.

Are costumed people in character?

You will encounter three types of costumed interpreters in the Historic Area: actor interpreters, guides, and artisans, known as tradespeople. Actor interpreters, such as those in the Revolutionary City program, portray people of the past and speak in character. You may also meet various actor interpreters, such as Thomas Jefferson and Gowan Pamphlet, as you tour around town. Guides, though dressed in colonial attire, speak from today. Guides lead tours, put things into context, help you plan, and point the way. You'll find guides at the entrances to as well as interpreting the sites. You may sometimes encounter guides who are not in colonial dress. Tradespeople are costumed and use eighteenth-century-type tools and techniques but speak from the twenty-first century.

Are there specialized walking tours that I can take?

Yes. In addition to orientation tours and tours of specific sites, there are other guided tours. Among the possibilities: Find out how gardens reflected eighteenth-century lifestyles and ideals. Visit the archaeological laboratories or collections preservation facilities. Learn about Colonial Williamsburg's modern stable and rare breeds program. In the evening, search for the ghosts of Williamsburg or meet some of Blackbeard's crew. These tours are typically sixty to ninety minutes long. The daytime tours are included with some of the admission passes but, due to limited space, require free reservations. The evening tours require the purchase of separate tickets. Make reservations and purchase tickets at any ticket sales location. Check "This Week" for offerings and schedules.

The Art Museums of Colonial Williamsburg offer tours related to their collections. These tours are typically thirty minutes. They are included in your museum admission. You do not need to make reservations. Check "This Week" for offerings and schedules.

Audio tours of the Historic Area and the Art Museums are also available.

Does Colonial Williamsburg offer group tours?

Yes. With advance planning, special tours are available for school and youth groups and for adult groups. For more information on group tours, call 1-800-228-8878 or go to www.history.org/history/teaching/grouptours/.

May I park in the Historic Area? Is there a bus system?

Automobiles are not permitted in the Historic Area, and there is limited parking surrounding the area. The best place to park is at the Visitor Center, where parking is free.

From 9 a.m. to 10 p.m. ticket holders may use the shuttle buses that travel between the Visitor Center and the Historic Area and stop at seven convenient locations around the Historic Area. All of the shuttle buses are wheelchair accessible.

Is the Historic Area accessible to persons with limited physical mobility?

Although the Visitor Center, hotels, restaurants, and shops are largely accessible, the nature of the Historic Area and its eighteenth-century architecture imposes certain restrictions on some guests. In many cases, staff members can help with accessibility or direct you to more-accessible sites. A limited number of folding wheelchairs are rented on a first-come, first-served basis from the Visitor Center. Wheelchair-accessible restrooms are located at the Visitor Center and in the Historic Area. See the map in "This Week" for locations. Colonial Williamsburg's shuttle buses between the Visitor Center and the Historic Area are wheelchair accessible.

Are there accommodations for persons with other physical limitations?
For guests with visual impairments, Colonial Williamsburg's Visitor Companion Braille Edition brochure is available at the Visitor Center. In *Williamsburg—The Story of a Patriot,* guests may make use of the headset sound track that describes the on-screen action. Ask the usher for assistance in setting up the headset. Guests with visual impairments may also make advance arrangements for an escort by contacting the visitor services coordinator at (757) 220-7645 or 800-246-2099. Licensed guide dogs are permitted in all of Colonial Williamsburg's buildings.

For guests with hearing impairments, headsets with adjustable volume control are available. The east theater has a rear-screen projection system that allows guests to see a captioned version of the film. Please ask the usher for assistance. Colonial Williamsburg will contract with one of several signing interpreters to accompany guests with hearing impairments through the Historic Area. Arrangements must be made two weeks in advance through the visitor services coordinator at (757) 220-7645 or 800-246-2099. Service animals are permitted in all buildings.

Admission tickets are discounted 50 percent to guests with disabilities. Tickets must be purchased at on-site ticket sales locations.

INDEX

IMAGE CREDITS

Chris Arace, 38, 40 left, 50–51; Scott Brown, 81 bottom right; Dave
Doody, back cover, 4, 14, 16–17, 20, 25, 27, 31, 34 right, 39, 40 right, 41,
42, 43 bottom, 47, 48, 49, 59, 60 right, 61 top left, 61 right, 62 bottom
left, 62 right, 63, 64, 66, 79 left, 83 right; Tom Green, 7 left, 8, 9, 10, 19,
22, 28, 29, 37, 44, 45, 46, 52 bottom right, 53 top left, 53 right, 54, 56, 57
left, 61 bottom left, 70, 74 right, 75, 76 bottom, 80 right, 81 top right, 82
top left, 84; Russell Kirk, 82 bottom left; Jeffrey Klee, 30; Mike Klemme,
76 top; Barbara Lombardi, 3, 11, 15, 18, 21, 24 right, 32, 35, 43 top, 50, 57
right, 58, 62 top left, 72, 73, 74 left, 82 right, 83 left; Hans Lorenz, 52 left,
52 top right, 53 bottom left; Maura McEvoy, front cover, 1, 5 left, 78; Kelly
Mihalcoe, 23, 24 left, 33, 60 left, 81 left; Erica Mueller, 65, 77 top; Victoria
Pearson, 55, 77 left, 77 right; Mark Tucker, 12, 13, 67, 79 right, 80 left; Lael
White, 34 left; John Whitehead, 5 right. Map by Richard McCluney.

THE COLONIAL WILLIAMSBURG FOUNDATION

The Colonial Williamsburg Foundation is a private, not-for-profit educational institution that receives no regular state or federal funding. The Foundation preserves and interprets the Historic Area; operates for-profit subsidiaries, including hotels, restaurants, convention facilities, and golf courses; and sells licensed products and reproductions.

In addition to the Historic Area, the Foundation also operates the DeWitt Wallace Decorative Arts Museum, the Abby Aldrich Rockefeller Folk Art Museum, Bassett Hall, and the John D. Rockefeller, Jr. Library.

Colonial Williamsburg actively supports history and citizenship education in schools and homes by engaging in a wide variety of educational outreach programs and activities. Through books, videotapes, recordings, and interactive digital media, Colonial Williamsburg presents the stories, words, and music of the eighteenth century.

The Idea of America is an interactive, fully digital, Web-based curriculum for high school students. Students learn lessons from history and the principles of American citizenship by exploring sixty-five case studies built around the nation's most important historical events, debating issues that changed America, exploring the perspectives of contemporary historians, and accessing primary source documents.

Electronic Field Trips transport students from across the country into American history, enabling them to meet people of the past and interact with them live about the individual choices they confronted as they worked to create the American republic.

Teacher-led student study visits to Williamsburg reveal the eighteenth century to hundreds of thousands of students each year.

The Williamsburg Teacher Institute, held on-site each year, along with workshops in school districts across the country, inspires thousands of teachers to use the Historic Area and Colonial Williamsburg resources to create innovative and engaging ways to teach about the past.

The Colonial Williamsburg Foundation needs and encourages tax-deductible gifts and bequests from all who treasure the Williamsburg experience. For more information, go to www.history.org/foundation/development, e-mail gifts@cwf.org, or call 1-888-CWF-1776.